THE ECLIPSE I CALL FATHER

THE ECLIPSE
I CALL FATHER

Essays on Absence

DAVID AXELROD

☙

Oregon State University Press   Corvallis

Library of Congress Cataloging-in-Publication Data

Names: Axelrod, David, 1958– author.
Title: The eclipse I call father : essays on absence / David Axelrod.
Description: Corvallis : Oregon State University Press, 2019.
Identifiers: LCCN 2018055309 | ISBN 9780870719691 (original trade pbk. :
    alk. paper)
Subjects: LCSH: Axelrod, David, 1958- | Axelrod, David, 1958—Childhood
    and youth. | Axelrod, David, 1958—Homes and haunts.
Classification: LCC PS3551.X39 Z46 2019 | DDC 814/.54—dc 3
LC record available at https://lccn.loc.gov/2018055309

♾ This paper meets the requirements of ANSI/NISO Z39.48-1992
    (Permanence of Paper).

First published in 2019 by Oregon State University Press
Printed in the United States of America

Oregon State University
OSU Press

Oregon State University Press
121 The Valley Library
Corvallis OR 97331-4501
541-737-3166 • fax 541-737-3170
www.osupress.oregonstate.edu

CONTENTS

ACKNOWLEDGMENTS

I wish to express my gratitude to the editors of the following publications in which these essays first appeared: *High Desert Journal*, "Note Left on a Mountain"; *Terrain: A Journal of the Built and Natural Environment*, "To Live as We Dream"; and *Serving House Journal*, "Boxing Lessons." In addition, thank you, constant companion, Jodi "Josefa" Varon. Also, many thanks to our children, Ezra and Joshua Axelrod, Tara Sun Vanacore, and David Restrepo. Thank you, Daneen Axelrod, for your strength and determination. Thank you, Christine Holbert, Christopher Howell, James Crews, Jennifer and Ian Boyden, Robert Stubblefield, Debra Earling, Ben Mitchell, Melissa Kwasny, and Piotr Florczyk, for your friendship and guidance. Thank you, Joe Wilkins, for your editorial insight. Finally, many thanks to Betty Mills, Sally Imhoff, Gayle Ormes Hawthorne, Richard McDaniel, Emily and Sandy Roth, Richard Kenton, Charles and Teresa Gills, Mary Rowland, Bruce Johnson, and last but not least, Kirsten Johnson and your aspirations.

We of the here-and-now are not for a moment satisfied in the world of time, nor are we bound in it; we are continually overflowing toward those who preceded us, toward our origin, and toward those who seemingly come after us. In that vast "open" world, all beings are—one cannot say "contemporaneous," for the very fact that time has ceased determines that they all are. Everywhere transience is plunging into the depths of Being....

—Rainer Maria Rilke

BASHŌ'S FROG

Ten years ago, we paddled away from a red beach just north of Willamette Pass in the Oregon Cascades, near the outlet of Waldo Lake, headwaters of the Willamette River. Our camp located us on the southern divide of the Columbia River watershed, where my constant companion, Josefa, and I have lived since 1980 and have traveled since marking its boundaries, tracing its lifelines, learning the gravity of its presence.

As we paddled away I already had been thinking about the great seventeenth century Japanese poet, Matsuo Bashō, who wrote this poem on a stormy day: "In the misty rain / Mount Fuji is veiled all day — / how intriguing!" Josefa and I had need of this gently comic insight the previous evening, when the weather turned awful. Like Bashō, we hadn't planned on encountering a late summer storm, but rather the far more conventional encounter travelers seek in mountain terrain. Nothing is so familiar as the sought-for confirmation of what others have seen and experienced in the fair-weather fantasy of travel. Nor is anything so delusional as that easily scotched expectation. Not seeing Mount Fuji is, Bashō reminds readers, every bit as interesting as seeing it. The same held true for us the night before.

1

Our kayak trip began not in late summer's balmy light air under calm blue heaven, but in storm that made our initial lake crossing an ordeal of choppy waves, headwinds, rain, and sleet stinging our faces. When I looked behind, between swells I saw Josefa, the bright vermilion banner of her long hair trailing in the wind as she fell farther behind in the three-foot waves. *How intriguing!*

Unable to light a fire in the cold rain, we sat in slickers on the overturned hulls of our kayaks, staring into mist, talking as rain fell more softly and finally ceased. The clouds lifted, sky appeared behind, and in the east, Jupiter rose along the ecliptic. The planet at that moment made its closest approach to Earth in decades, appearing so bright it cast shadows on shore. Melancholy receding, we went to our tent under a sky full of stars.

As I paddled from shore thinking of Bashō that next morning, the cones of nearby Cascade volcanoes came into view to the north, gleaming with fresh snow. Mount Bachelor particularly bore remarkable resemblance to iconic Japanese landscape paintings of Mount Fuji.

A quarter mile from shore, I let my kayak drift in the still water, and a tiny frog—also crossing the lake—rose to the surface beside the boat. It was a pale green Pacific tree frog, common throughout the Northwest, and in Oregon dispersed from the coast over the Cascades into eastern Oregon, where I often listen to its springtime choruses. The Pacific tree frog may live in diverse habitats, but it typically doesn't stray more than a few feet from the body of water it lives in or around. Was the frog intrepid, desperate, confused? At that point, given his direction of travel, the frog already had exceeded that typical distance from shore a hundred times or more, with a mile yet to go to reach the other side. Was the scale of that little frog's journey then at least six hundred times the scale of my own—a journey equivalent to my traveling not a mile and a half, but nine hundred miles? What was over there on the east shore of Waldo Lake this frog preferred to the west, and that he would undergo such an epic ordeal to find? What is purpose, time, space, here, there, or elsewhere to a frog? Where he begins, where he ends the brief duration of his life— what difference could it possibly make? In his frog brain, what is the duration of any event? What, for that matter, is an event?

The most famous frog is Bashō's frog sitting beside an old pond—*splash*! It's sometimes referred to as a perfectly achieved haiku, simultaneously literal and metaphorically resonant, the embodiment of the poet's poetics of ordinary things and his Buddhism. It also seemed then a proper rejoinder to all the questions I posed: that frog was just being a frog fully in the moment of its mindful froggy-ness, without any concerns about what has been or will be. I was inclined to take a lesson from this: act naturally as any self-respecting frog.

Frogs and humans are not quite the same, are they? That frog probably didn't think about me in quite the same way as I thought about him. And besides frogs, who wishes to achieve this enlightened state of frog-iety? All the same, I wasn't invisible either. As in Ed Panar's book of photographs, *Animals That Saw Me*, that frog was another animal that saw me. In the end, we have in common the likelihood that what a frog wishes for is as vulnerable as human wishes, but with this caveat: we're leaving a record of this melancholy fact. Bashō's poem is a happy example of the same. It surely has proven itself far more durable than either his or the frog's life. From the (admittedly speculative) frog's point of view, I could well suffer a judgment for a blindness he does not share of a catastrophe that we do.

Even at the time of our encounter on at Waldo Lake, I was aware that the nighttime choruses of my youth, like the choruses along Mill Creek where I first lived in Oregon, have grown fainter, if they aren't stilled altogether. All indications are that a sixth global extinction is underway, driven largely by civilization. Amphibians have survived four extinctions prior to the one that is ongoing, but an assessment for the National Academy of Sciences conducted by David B. Wake and Vance T. Vredenburg warns, "Among the groups most affected by the current extinction are the amphibians." Drawing on the different predictive warming scenarios, Wake and Vredenburg write, mountain amphibian extinction "is now an empirical fact."

In one weird passage from their conclusion, in which they discuss the "extrinsic forces, such as global warming and increased climate variability," the authors address human beings in the third person: "But we can be sure that behind all these activities is one weedy species, *Homo sapiens*, which has unwittingly achieved the ability to directly affect its own fate and that of most of the other species on the planet. It is an intelligent species . . ." Bashō himself couldn't be any more gently ironic than that. Still, I'm not quite so willing to grant human beings either naiveté or intelligence, as who among us isn't aware, every time we turn ignition keys, purchase food, turn up furnaces or turn on air conditioners, that we're drenching the planet in the toxic sludge of fossil fuels?

At first, I tried to lift the frog onto my paddle and give him a lift, a gesture that proved foolish and futile. The frog spent his energy trying instead to avoid my affectionate attentions, descending into the water, resurfacing only to resume his obscure quest. Finally, I left him alone and watched. He kicked his legs and moved forward a couple inches, floated, kicked again, and moved a couple inches more. After another minute of this, he rested, drifting backward, erasing his progress; then, carefully readjusting his compass to stay on course, he began to kick again, determined to arrive somewhere, someday, on that far-off forested shore, for purposes as obscure as my own.

ACCRETIONS OF ABSENCE

Last winter was unusually warm here in the western outliers of the Rocky Mountains. Under ordinary circumstances, we would expect—and some few might even welcome—the cold and snow. In their absence, our local dependence on long, cold, snowy winters followed by cool, cloudy springs is evident in falling river levels and aquifers—the primary sources of our irrigated lives in the Grande Ronde Valley in northeastern Oregon, between the Blue and Wallowa Mountains.

A hard winter is also called a "good snow year," and is something to celebrate rather than dread. In a good snow year, mid-elevations between three thousand and six thousand feet could easily hold snowpack several feet deep as much as a month after spring equinox. A good snow year is when we can "ski over Mount Emily" on April Fool's Day—a ten-mile loop that begins at thirty-seven hundred feet and tops out at six thousand. It has been many years now since we last skied that loop in April, much less in winter. In this we recognize climate predictions coming true: local mid-elevation snowpacks seem to be diminishing.

In a good snow year, the higher elevations might hold upward of ten feet of snow well into July, with north-facing mountain cirques never entirely melting out. An example of this preferred extreme was an enormous snowpack that formed five years ago, after a series of slightly-colder-than-normal late storms turned an otherwise mediocre snowpack into a record one. Hiking at eight thousand feet in July that year, we encountered ten feet of snow, with only the tops of trees poking a few feet above the snowbound Lakes Basin.

The effects of this good hydrological fortune seemed significant. We maintained a groundwater surplus up until the most recent year. In the intervening years, there were few if any one-hundred-degree-Fahrenheit days in summer, which we had grown accustomed to in the previous decade and will likely experience again soon. Under these favorable conditions, foothills remained green a month longer in summer. The wild berry crops were so numerous, locals enjoyed one of our oldest and most eagerly awaited egalitarian rituals—picking huckleberries—beginning July fourth and continuing through Labor Day.

These were fat years. Intermittent streams ran longer in summer, rivers colder and fuller. Because of efforts tribes and government agencies made to restore habitat and river complexity, salmon flourished. Though I once observed descendants of Chief Looking Glass fishing in a tributary of the lower Grande Ronde River that was their forebear's ancestral home, last summer local tribal members fished for sockeye in the upper Grande Ronde River for the first time in my memory. It seemed possible that old rituals of return could be reestablished, that our little sliver of world could be restored to its previous and preferred stability.

Wolves, moose, and even wolverines, all long absent, began reappearing in the mountains. If there were forest fires, they were put out within hours and seldom grew larger than a couple acres. The clear cuts and fire scars from the last drought during the Reagan years, when logs were shipped to Asia and national forestlands were decimated, were verdant with dense young growth of aspen, pine, and fir. The snowfields below Glacier Peak in the nearby wilderness filled the cirque above Glacier Lake, allowing the opportunity to glissade no less than a thousand feet from the ridge to the green lakeshore. Under such conditions you might have allowed yourself to believe life here on this western margin of the Rockies paradisiacal.

That's the difference between a single degree of Fahrenheit warmer or colder around the freezing mark. The apparent stasis of averages, though, has shifted. A botanist who moved here at the same time we did has kept a record of last spring and first fall frosts for each of the last thirty years. It's a record of her sheltered backyard garden on the lower slopes of Rooster Peak. First and last frosts vary around the valley, but my friend and colleague's record provides local evidence of an effect of global warming: the last frost averages a month earlier today than when we arrived. It was common then to find ourselves outside covering young plants well into June. A local proverb warns not to plant tomatoes until the snow has melted on Mount Emily, typically during the first or second week in June. Today, we can plant tomatoes in early May.

In the past, on my constant companion's birthday just before Midsummer Eve, we often found ourselves in heavy sweaters or down parkas. Summers as I recall them often were punctuated by two cold snaps accompanied by mountain snows: one around July fourth and the other during the third week in August, the latter coinciding with our wedding anniversary, when we often woke at dawn inside a snowbound tent. Our first summer here, I planted an acre of squash and tomatoes, thinking to supplement our income. Frost destroyed the entire crop on August twenty-fifth. Three decades later, the first autumn frost comes as late as early November.

My botanist friend's attention—precise and ritualized in seasonal durations in place—is a sliver of information about conditions of life here. We call our habitation a lifetime and imagine it somehow a sufficient sum of meaning and insight, though ours may be nearer to the experience of a box-elder bug—whose life spans a year—than it is to the whitebark pine—whose life spans centuries.

᠈᠊᠊ᡐ

It's a clear day in late October, a week since we put the garden to sleep and tilled under the debris. We're hiking the Angel Peak-Black Lake Traverse. A week from now, enough snow will have fallen to complicate travel, at least above seven thousand feet. No chance of snow today though: below freezing in the sheltered canyons and basins, bluebird skies above, honey-colored sunlight beaming at a low angle through the trees, and long shadows radiating a calm, blue chill. The moisture in the ground froze overnight, wicking up into brittle honeycombs of ice that crunch underfoot. Ice formed over pools in streams and along the edges of lakes.

The Angel Peak-Black Lake Traverse sounds a lot grander than the reality. It's not a long hike. Maybe four or five miles, though because of the steepness, some exposure, and the elevation on the ridge above eight thousand feet, it takes a few hours. There's a little scrambling through boulders to reach the ridge. By noon, we're descending.

In the pass between Angel Peak and Gunsight Mountain, I wait for Josefa, who pokes her way down the steep slope, following a goat trail across sedge, scree, and brittle granite that's not quite sand yet. Though we've come this way no fewer than five times in the previous twenty-five years, I'm surprise by a tumbled-over, dry-stacked wall of stones and a long tongue of tailings below a rockface. Soon, we're standing side-by-side to marvel at a rectangular opening rough-cut into the base of the granite. The mine entrance disappears around a corner of the wall, daylight fading to black just a few steps inside. A cool damp breath comes out of

the rocks. We stand with our hands pressed against the flat surface of granite as if we are Ali Baba and it might swing open and
lure us inside.

As it turns out, there isn't much of an opening into the stone.
The miner went in ten feet and stopped. Ewart M. Baldwin's *Oregon Geology* explains that this granite was exposed during the Late
Jurassic and mineralization occurred later in geologic time, during
the Tertiary. Vast as the time this rock took to form and move to
the surface—two hundred million years—the duration of the
late nineteenth-century gold rush it provoked lasted only a few
decades.

What attracted this miner's attention were two cracks in the
granite full of quartz crystals—one has large iron-stained crystals
in a crumbling sandy matrix; the other, deeper in the cut, appears
to have similarly large, but less brittle, clearer crystals. The latter
seam is peppered with bluish-green flecks of oxidized copper
mixed into quartz. In both, the crystals grew from the edges of
granite into the opening crack. Neither seam is any wider than a
fist. If you break off a chunk and hold it in your palm, the crystals
embedded in stone have the unnerving appearance of the deracinated jawbones and broken teeth of a nightmarish werewolf.

After half an hour of deciding what rocks to load into my
pack (a lot, it turns out), we descend from the pass, sidestepping
through talus and scrub to Black Lake. Once on the trail, we begin
talking again, and the topic turns to the mystified accounting we
seem prone to as we've aged. First, how many times does one pass
a place before becoming remotely aware it's a *place*? What are the
distinctive features, what narrative evident in the details? Five
times in twenty-five years we passed that crack in the rocks and
only on the sixth glimpsed that trace of the miner's passage from a
century prior to our own.

Another, grimmer accounting is the not-so-astonishing recognition of how much time has elapsed since we first made the tra-

verse in 1995 with young children. That is humbling enough, but there is also the corollary awareness of another melancholy fact. We will not very likely be making the traverse with grandchildren in another twenty-five years.

We cross a footbridge, and I say what I have been rehearsing as we descended from the pass: "Time isn't as much a limiting factor as it seems." Spoken aloud, that sounds improbable, but I won't be deterred by my companion's skepticism. We pass through these places, follow these same trails for a generation or more, and these places and trails accumulate us, even in our absence, just as houses accumulate occupants.

"There is a kind of eternity here," I say, "and we're participating in it even as we sense we're exiting its presence."

Josefa steps aside and turns to me. Looking into her blue eyes is like peering into portals of clear sky. "Are you okay?"

⌀

Last spring, I reread the thirty-one-syllable *waka* of the medieval Japanese poet, Saigyō. Two poems appear on facing pages, in English and *romaji*. I read two to four poems a day, though I missed a day or two here and there. Saigyō lived in a turbulent era of Japanese history, the court collapsing after three hundred fifty years of political and social stability. In the poems he seems chronically saddened by decay and corruption. In his early twenties, he retreated from secular life, "placing himself," as translator William R. LaFleur writes, "in probative situations in which strength and endurance could be tested." We often find Saigyō crossing perilous mountain ridges or rivers swollen with rain. He travels the territory where human efforts seem futile, our effects vulnerable, transitory, and woven into the physical world whose conditions are catastrophic. The only certainty in this terrain is vulnerability before the forces of nature. "Penniless woodcutter," one poem begins, "Managed to get for himself a hut / Hanging on a steep slope / And as boundary mark a gem, / A jade-green young willow tree."

Doomed as the woodcutter's efforts may be, his desire to dwell, to cultivate, to leave a trace of himself or his household in refuge and willow expresses an aspiration toward permanence, despite his poverty. Saigyō is melancholy, but also full of gratitude for the fragile gesture of that "gem," the living, cultivated thing that wants only to go on living, like the woodcutter, in that place. A poem such as this becomes a permanent part of our conflicted human geography, a surrogate dwelling at which we may pause in every generation since Saigyō's and his subject's disappearance. Despite the futility of the impoverished woodcutter's desire, a trace of his existence and its complex or contradictory meanings endure on the page. We stop, glance at the steep hillside now grown up in weeds, the hut simultaneously present and absent. The wood-cutter and the wandering poet have created a place, an ongoing event, art and life making peace with one another.

Then I left for Germany, and Saigyō remained behind. Return-ing eight weeks later, I resumed my practice and spent a moment most mornings wandering slowly through the mountains and along the riverbanks of twelfth-century Japan. Poem after poem celebrates blossoming trees and full moons, images of transience, change, and the forbearance of the enlightened mind maintain-ing its equipoise in Saigyō's "withering world." Small consola-tion these philosophical commonplaces. Still, we recognize the tremendous dignity in this paradoxical desire to be present, this intention to dwell, in all the senses of which the duration of life resists the impermanence of lives.

~❧~

"Paintings are static," John Berger writes in his essay "Once," con-trasting art to the flow of lived time. There exists in art a breach between the life of the art object and the life of the one observing it, of the one creating it, and of the original model—a moment that was and continues to be. Art, we admit, is more like a tree than its makers. Art moves through time and space slowly, experiencing a greater portion of eternity than we ever will as individuals. Berger, however, proposes a critique of linear time, as opposed to older, cyclic conceptions of time he wants to extol. Insofar as paintings are places we visit, and because paintings have been accumulating gazes of those passing before them for centuries, inviting us to return, to dwell closer than the guard in the corner finds comfortable. Meanwhile, art gazes back, evaluating our lives, the openness of hearts and minds—and because of all of this, it's almost impossible to regard paintings as static.

A painting, like Saigyō's poem, is a physical place, an ongoing event. It accumulates vast amounts of anonymous human time and longing. Should we pause long enough to sense the power of the accumulated past, present before us even in its absence, we experience something like ecstasy.

We imagine the world we inhabit in much the same way as we've looked at great works of art, hastening through the Paleolithic galleries to "see it all," taking snapshots and selfies for social media to prove, conclusively, our existence is every bit as transitory and meaningless as we fear. Until, for whatever blessed reason, we pause in wonder before the Titian, thunderstruck by the flesh and hair of Mary Magdalene. In the coming decade, my constant companion and I will seek out that one painting again and again, stand or sit before it in different cities, read about it in books, and forget to reach for our smartphones.

This past winter, I drove alone one morning into the Elkhorns in search of snow, which seems to reside now only at higher elevations. I listened to the Icelandic cellist Hildur Guðnadóttir perform her composition, *Without Sinking*, whose "aim . . . [is] to create a feeling of breath with a bow on string." That "feeling of breath" recalled a gallery show I attended several years ago, in which the artist, Jelena Berenc, a young mother then, displayed drawings she made as she sat with her sleeping newborn—long wavering lines in graphite on soft cotton paper, the duration of her newborn's breaths, one after another. Berenc described these drawings as "durational, repetitional, excessive and endurance drawings." A striking body of work, for sure, minimalist at first encounter, but upon consideration, maximalist and monumental, opening toward the vastness of life contained in the place the drawing creates, where we try to match our own breath to that of a child's whose future far exceeds our own.

As I listened to Guðnadóttir's music, I also thought of Morton Feldman, who must be one of Guðnadóttir's predecessors, as Agnes Martin's meditative, horizontal grids are a likely predecessor of Berenc. In Feldman's *Durations I-V,* time and its tone, as is often the case in his compositions, slow and expand both in breadth and depth, searching out the eternity in the moment of a sustained note. Be here in this place and be still, the music asks us. Here in the duration of a tone is an opportunity to live a while without dying.

Berger puts it another way, though it seems that he has a similar thing in mind: "The deeper the experience of a moment, the greater the accumulation of experience. This is why the moment is lived as longer. The dissipation of the time-flow is checked. The lived *durée* isn't a question of length but of depth or density."

What is that depth or density if not the accretion of absence?

❧

Josefa and I once lived briefly on a broad terraced mountainside in Andalusia. We walked the ancient trails on that mountainside for an entire month, following herds of Nubian goats from pasture to pasture. The canyon below us had been occupied many thousands of years before civilization arrived with its einkorn and threshing circles paved with moon-reflecting mica flagstones. Our first human ancestors walked out of Africa onto that mountainside. Our month there was miserable, cold, and snowy. After a week of burning olive wood in a smoky tin stove, we'd failed to raise the heat of that cavernous seven-year-old house enough so as not to see our breath.

Below the house, an ancient mill crumbled into ruins beside the river Romans spanned with an arched bridge of quarried stone. The weedy, cobbled, Roman road climbed toward the opposite ridge and the trade routes of the imperium. That former Berber village now consisted of thirty-five connected stucco houses that seemed like a deserted beehive. Only at night, a light burned at the interior of those cells, just a faint and distant glow on a small windowpane.

One morning, walking that former imperial road along the south side of the river, we were surprised by an Iberian ibex ram asleep beneath a gorse. We froze midstep and said nothing. Face to face with something wild and elemental, we assumed at any moment he would leap to his feet, shake himself alert, challenge us to back down. We held our breath as time deepened and grew denser all around us. The Sierra Nevada snows lingered high above, and below lay the coast, Africa across the sea, and the whole continent beyond. The ibex, however, didn't rise, because he wasn't asleep, but dead. Yet another surprise followed upon our alert attention: a kind of dread, as though we'd stumbled on evidence of something forbidden. We looked around to see if anyone was watching, then we turned back to the corpse. His big, milky, slatted eye gazed blankly at the Andalusian sky. A full curl of horns, a thick tawny winter coat, and no sign at all of what killed him.

It was one of the first warm days; snowmelt swelled the river, rock thrushes sang off in the scrub, and the rock face we stood beneath sang its loud devotional echo of the river's shimmering voice below. Across the canyon a goatherd whistled to his dog who moved Nubians from one paddock to another. On sunny south-facing terraces, the almond trees seemed suddenly to have burst into pink blossom.

I can't fully account for why a moment like that is so resonate with strangeness and wonder, though when one lives abroad, the perception of the depth and density of time in place often seems more readily accessible than it does at home. For the residents of such a village in the Sierra Nevada, you have to admit, there is likely considerably less strangeness and wonder. Everyone else probably knew about the ram, how it died and when, or who murdered it. Yet for us, the oddness of that tiny, impoverished village hanging off the terraced mountainside, and its mythical past as a refuge for Moorish princes to whom sorrowful nightingales sang—the presence everywhere of what was absent and the mystery of that absence—demanded accounting, an invented narrative. Factual or fanciful, it hardly mattered; sojourners like us are forced at every moment to explain the world to ourselves.

The more pointed question, though, is posed on return to the familiar world of one's home. How shall we perceive the familiar as possessed of the same densities and depths of strangeness and wonder as that moment on the Roman road? Privileged as we are to visit places that the permanent residents often can't leave, we return home to the same predicament as they who never depart.

How can we learn to look at the familiar as if it were occupied now and forever by the accumulated presences of the past that only appear on the surface as absent? To live in this manner is to dwell in gratitude for a world full of astonishing resonances. The depth and density of presence in the world is so powerful that there is no place in, on, or of this earth that does not see us for who and what we are.

⌀

The dream insisted on the perdurance of life, replicating itself beyond the borders of one lifetime into another. In that dream, we died, became smoke, lay as ashes on a mountain of ash, and then, miraculously restored, walked upstream on opposite banks of the Grande Ronde River in cool twilight.

Despite the sorrows that accompanied us, we toiled our way back toward human form, determined to abandon neither this place nor one another, constant companions calling back and forth across the rapids to assure each other we remained steadfast. Then we stood side by side in a grove of old trees. So old were those trees, we knew they had remained unmolested since humans emerged into this world. A dozen people linking outstretched arms couldn't have reached all the way around the trunks. High above us, heavy and massive, the limbs hovered in the air, spreading their wide, entwined canopy. We'd lived absent from that grove so long that we stood in awe of the strangeness of its shelter.

How could that grove seem simultaneously odd and familiar—a place we knew of from more than one point in time, and at no point in our own? Perhaps it was a memory inherent to our species. Perhaps these trees were the forest Humbaba guarded before the assault by Gilgamesh and his hairy friend, Enkidu. Perhaps that forest persists, an atavistic memory fraught with shadows of anxiety and subsequent loss. The grove gleamed full of light, honey-rich, amber light of autumn. Somehow, it had escaped the violence of history.

The tree represents "life without end," Mircea Eliade wrote, as it perpetually restores itself in time, and becomes emblematic of an "absolute reality." Had we found our way in that dream back from the absolute reality of death into the absolute reality of life, or were they one and the same? That liminal grove didn't conceal the terrors of history, from which we only recently returned as from a fog, but revealed a durable, persistent, even stubborn joy.

Fully a decade after waking from that dream of old trees, we walked fully awake into the same grove, some remnant of it anyway, along the South Fork of the Imnaha. As we descended into the canyon from the north, we passed uncommonly tall stands of Douglas fir. One fir, recently struck by lightning and partially burned, had been sawed down by a fire crew that quickly contained the blaze to a thirty-foot-wide circle of charred grasses and forbs, and the old fir at the center. We counted several inches of rings then multiplied by the approximate radius: five hundred years. In the river bottom, though, the old larches, even broader and taller, were so much like that calming dream from a decade before, I stood in the grove, dumbfounded. First, at the recognition of how seldom one sees old trees, much less a whole grove of old trees. But also in gratitude for the uncanny good fortune to find my way in waking life into that archetypal dream whose source remained a discoverable reality.

❧

Soon after leaving those larch groves along the South Forth of the Imnaha River last year, we celebrated Rosh Hashanah—the Days of Awe, during which we account for our lives and the worthiness of those lives continuing until another harvest.

The first night we break and share the eternal braid of bread that rises in the shape of a crown, the Crown of Life, whose crust is covered with sesame seeds representing the infinity of particular things. To remind us of the sweetness of life, we slice apples from the old homesteader's trees our friends restored in their orchard and dip these apples from another century in honey gathered from the same orchard.

And now yet another year has come around to Rosh Hashanah. Tonight, we will celebrate the sweetness of life and another successful harvest. We will load the table with foods that we and our friends have grown and prepared. That's reason enough to celebrate through at least a dozen millennia after the Ice Age glaciers and floods began to recede, and human beings began to alter earth's ecology on a global scale. How strange to celebrate this ritual now, to feel the full weight of gratitude in our hearts and minds for all that shadow world, haunting us still.

The six-year-old boy seated next to me at table, blowing the shofar for the first time, or at least the six-thousandth time—how can I meet his eyes without feeling ashamed of the world we will leave him? Or my unborn grandchild, who on the other side of the continent also hears the shofar tonight for the first time inside his mother's womb? How strange the High Holidays will seem to them without the promise of snow, the acidified oceans smelling of death, fields blighted by drought, the coasts drowned by flood—the gentler, richer world before their own having joined the accretions of absence. How strange then to remember us at this table full of riches, and how little we did to ensure a different outcome for them and their impoverished world of refugees.

Just so, the Days of Awe return between the New Year and Yom Kippur, the Day of Atonement, when we ask forgiveness of the creator (whoever or whatever that absence might be) for our sins of malice or indifference, and fast in the hopes that our names will be inscribed in the Book of Life for the duration of another year. During that year may we learn the full dimensions of gratitude. Maybe then, maybe next year or maybe the year after, we will open our hands to refugees and secure life for someone else's child, someone we will never know, as we will have become the flavor of the food, sustaining others in a future better than the one we now imagine.

TO LIVE AS WE DREAM

My parents' house, which they built in 1960, was a tiny, white, Modernist tract house constructed from sturdy materials, trimmed in green, with clean, plain lines, and overall an expression of practical, affordable design. Situated at the middle of a crabgrass lot, it fronted the bucolically named Pleasant Place, one lot north of forests and marshes that on summer nights erupted in choruses of frogs. Standing on my bed and looking through the casement window screen (why were windows always placed so high on the walls of houses built in that era?), I looked out into darkness hallucinatory with fireflies and the Milky Way. In a recent dream, I moved back into that house decorated as it was in 1960: sleek Danish-style furniture, Fauvist and Cubist prints, the RCA Victor console stereo with its collection of LPs by Johnny Mathis, Peggy Lee, Sammy Davis Jr., and Nat King Cole. The accretions of over fifty intervening years of my life fit comfortably, if improbably, within the dream of that tiny house.

Early in his classic exploration of the home, *The Poetics of Space*, Gaston Bachelard dwells on the way the intimacy of childhood spaces persists throughout our lives, especially in reveries. Lost in daydreams, we don't so much inhabit the memory of our childhood home; instead, we live in its absence as we once dreamed in its presence. I'm inclined to agree with this, though it's the houses not lived in as a child but visited and departed with an unusual feeling of well-being that interest me now.

That tract house my young parents built, and occupied as briefly as their marriage endured, always seemed untidy and cramped, at first full of manias, then a long bleak period of grief. It was quite the opposite of the houses of some of the family and friends we visited. Those houses always seemed aglow with the calm light of a November afternoon just before it begins to snow. Or in the oppressive humidity of an Ohio summer, those rooms remained cool, full of shadows the color of polished oak. Without exception, those were Craftsman houses.

The heavy front doors or foyers of Craftsman houses open into living rooms with large stone hearths, the many-lighted and beveled-glass windows, dark and heavily grained woodwork, built-in cabinets with glass-paneled doors, dining rooms with large bay windows, and the sight-lines of one room opening into another, creating the illusion of spacious luxury. The walls above the wainscoting were often painted in pale green that contrasted with the dark-grained woodwork, intended to harmonize with the natural world. These were houses designed with such a deep sense of spatial balance, intimacy, and structural integrity it's hard to believe today that they were the typical homes of many working-class and lower-middle-class families in my hometown. That such houses could be purchased as kits and built quickly, often for less than a thousand dollars, is mind-blowing.

After more than a generation of shipping manufacturing jobs overseas, wage stagnation, the destruction of labor unions, and tax redistribution that transfers wealth upwards, today such working- and lower-middle-class families are lucky to be living in trailers or suburban ticky-tacky; lucky, that is, if they aren't living in their cars, the homeless and dispossessed refugees of post-modernity.

Many of these same Craftsman houses now sell for as much as half a million dollars, even during the Great Recession we're only now coming to the end of. At the height of its popularity, though, such architectural design was an expression of socialist idealism and respect; namely, the belief that all segments of society had access to domestic space that, at least in its design, nurtured the souls of its inhabitants and brought them into greater harmony with the natural world.

That's a lot of wishful thinking, and it would be folly to imagine such an ahistorical reality existed; but as an ideal, as an aspiration, I'm all for it now, and even as a child, sensed its power. In her survey of social reform aesthetics, "House and Home in the Arts and Crafts Era: Reforms for Simpler Living," Cheryl Robertson quotes Kate Greenleaf Locke from a 1907 issue of *House & Garden*: "[Craftsman design] appeals to a wide circle and several classes. . . . there is yet in its atmosphere a delightful flavor of Bohemianism and the liberty and originality that camp life and studio life permits." Robertson concludes: "the bungalow combined the attributes of taste, rusticity, and economy . . . [and applied them] to the villa, farmhouse, and cottage . . . [a] democratization of domestic architecture [that is] evidenced in 'classless' bungalows." That's surely a more thoughtful idealism about how we might occupy space and has proven far more durable than most contemporary, postmodern spaces. Many corporate spaces and post-war apartment blocks, by contrast, particularly those remnant examples of Brutalism, compound error upon error and become, in the critique of Christopher Alexander, forbidding "reservoirs" of stress. Such poured concrete, bunker-like buildings seem designed to allow for little else than the possibility of siege.

◦

In the summer of 2002, I visited a friend in Billings, Montana, who lived in a neighborhood like many in the American West, dating from the 1920s and full of Craftsman houses. His house, located near a corner on a narrow lot along a leafy street was, he stipulated, a "Craftsman cottage." Inside were two bedrooms in which the original family raised five children. There were a multitude of kitchen cabinets, built-in bookcases in the half-walls between dining and living rooms, and wainscoting and hardwood floors. Filled with his sturdy antique furniture, it felt cozy inside despite the enormity of the Great Plains stretching north, south, and east for a thousand miles beyond the horizons.

During that visit, we rose early one day and drove to the mountains above Red Lodge. The light that July morning in the Rocky Mountains filtered down through lodgepole pines. We slowed as we passed through a cluster of structures, a pre–Great Depression "camp" below the Beartooth Plateau, where we intended to spend our day hiking. Scattered throughout the dense trees above and below the dusty road were a dozen or so tidy cabins and outbuildings constructed from materials available in the surrounding forests: unpeeled pine logs, river cobbles, and mud. The screened windows, porches, and doorways, and the rolled green asbestos roofing, recalled an era deep in the past, the world of my grandfather's coming of age during the Great Depression. It was a moment when citizens briefly shared a belief in our egalitarian national destiny. Call this again what it is: an ahistorical claim. Nevertheless, it's the lens through which I was taught to perceive my country's ideals, if not its reality.

We passed by the camp so quickly, all I can recall with any clarity was a single fastidious cabin just above the road on the passenger side. It seemed more like a playhouse than a cabin. It was so tiny that it would have allowed just enough room for a bunk, maybe a bench, and a small stove on the front porch. Whoever had spent summers living there, I imagined, spent most of their days outdoors. When these cabins were built, only the most rudimentary road or, more likely, trail would have existed. Getting into that canyon would have required a good deal more effort than we made driving there in little more than an hour from Billings. These were very resourceful sojourners. Whoever they were, I immediately assumed I wanted to know them.

That tiny camp in the immensity of a Montana canyon, like my friend's cottage back in Billings, seemed an unlikely confluence of egalitarian ideals and domestic intimacy, a reservoir of calm and comradeship, at ease with the natural world into which it was unobtrusively tucked away.

　　　　　　　　　　　　　　❧

Daydreaming later about that cabin, I thought I had stumbled upon something like the playhouse that my great uncle had constructed for his daughters in Ohio. It had a little picket fence and gate. Lilac and rose of Sharon shaded the screened porch, inside of which there were diminutive chairs and a settee, just the right size for a child. Surrounding the porch was a bed full of yellow iris and a border made of whitewashed cobbles. Her father filled the playhouse with furniture he made: an entire kitchen, a parlor, and a tiny bedroom. My cousin Nancy seemed, like Alice in the Tenniel illustration, hunched over, a bit overgrown for those rooms by the time I stepped across its threshold, but never mind, the sunny kitchen with its many cabinets and cool shady parlor were enchanting. We sat, pretending to serve afternoon tea in miniature porcelain cups. It seemed what civilized people in books would do of an English afternoon. The origin of such decorum seems mystifying, as we weren't bookish and knew of no such adults who were. Perhaps we responded to the wholesome genius of her father's design? Out the back door of the kitchen we stepped directly into a garden full of vegetables that were surrounded by raspberry canes and a double loop, ornamental wire fence such as was ubiquitous then. Nancy's father died, and eventually that little playhouse fell into disrepair, as did the farm, as did Nancy's family, her brothers degenerating into the cable TV-fueled ideologies of rural racism and resentments that counter my stubborn ahistorical dream of socialist harmony.

By now the playhouse that enchanted me is gone, and probably no one gives it much thought, its ruins buried under briars. Though, perhaps, with a bow to Bachelard, Nancy lives in its absence now as once she dreamed in its presence? Surely it has not vanished from reveries such as I experienced during the ten years since I first laid eyes on that camp deep in the forests of south-central Montana, my whole entourage of family, friends, and houses we inhabited accompanying me as we drove into the Beartooths? As I imagined it, Camp Senia (whose name I found on a map of the Beartooths) became a place where it was still possible to live as we dream.

⚬

Returning to Camp Senia accompanied by my constant companion in June 2011, circumstances forced me to admit that what I remembered about the camp was little more than fantasy. As she drove us up the West Fork of Rock Creek, I wondered if perhaps I had forgotten where exactly I visited a decade earlier. She asked if anything looked familiar. I couldn't be sure. *Everything* had changed.

For one, the canyon had burned. Mile after mile we wound through bare, scorched tree trunks that climbed steeply from the creek bottom to the ridges. When we came suddenly upon the cabins, it was as though I'd never seen that place. The tiny cabin above the road was there, but not the same. It no longer stood in soft green kinnikinnick and ground pine, dappled by the golden light of my forested summer reveries. Rather, it sat in the stark, flat, wide-awake glare of a shadowless noon. Few living trees remained. The forest floor had been reduced to just a few rough sedges, shrubs, and bare mineral soil. The tiny cabin stood next to a larger cabin I didn't recall.

A knot of people stood along the road talking below that larger cabin. Several of them helped an elderly man into the passenger seat of a pickup truck. Here was another surprise: people!

Somehow, despite having claimed to want to meet imaginary occupants a decade before, I subsequently failed to imagine that anyone lived in Camp Senia. This was a complication. Though we spent the morning in the county historical society's archives reading about the construction of the camp and ownership of the cabins, the reality of continued occupation obviously hadn't sunk in. Suddenly overcome by shyness, we waved awkwardly and continued to the trailhead at the end of the road, where we sat and wondered, a little absurdly, what to do.

That the canyon had burned came as little surprise.

Lodgepole pine is ubiquitous throughout the American West. The scent of its hot pitch is one of the familiar forest scents of summer. But lodgepole also has a brief fire cycle, burning roughly once during a human lifetime. The tree's reproductive cycle evolved to require fire to open its cones and drop its seeds to a forest floor where competition has been reduced, literally, to ashes. Fire suppression, though, resulted in dense stands of lodgepole that have accumulated huge fuel loads on the forest floor, increasing the likelihood of catastrophic fires that burn hotter without intervention.

In late July 2008, a wildfire whose origin was never verified swept down the West Fork of Rock Creek Canyon and through Camp Senia. The Cascade Fire, as it was officially known, spread quickly to over ten thousand acres and resulted in the emergency evacuation of the entire area. As fire approached, residents had little time to vacillate over what to take with them. One summer resident described the awful sound of fast-approaching fire to a reporter for the *Billings Gazette*. He described it "as a low, throaty roar" that haunted him even more than the sight of flames crowning in trees.

The effort in the 1980s to create a Camp Senia Historic District and add the cabins to the National Register of Historic Places likely paid off, as firefighters worked fast to soak the camp in fire retardant foam and save the cabins and outbuildings from oncoming flames. Only two cabins and a few smaller structures were destroyed, which seems miraculous, given the density of the forest and the available dry fuels.

"Well," Josefa said as we sat at the trailhead, "what do you want to do?"

It had been my idea, after all, to drive seven hundred miles to see these cabins; surely this was no time to behave shyly about intruding on people's privacy. We drove back to the camp, parked, got out, and walked over to the knot of people who were now waving good-bye to the elderly man in the pickup truck, whose younger relatives were driving him back to Billings. I walked over and asked, "Would it be bad form to walk down through the camp and look at the cabins?"

"Those cabins are on public property," a woman about our age said. "You're free to walk here wherever you wish. It's yours after all." What she said wasn't entirely true; the cabins were most certainly not ours, but she was in earnest. There wasn't an ounce of irony or guile in what she said. And as none there contradicted her, one might assume they agreed with this assessment. When we explained our reason for visiting the camp, she formally introduced herself and offered a guided walking tour.

◆

The camp was conceived by a young couple, Alfred Croonquist, son of a Swedish merchant in nearby Red Lodge, and Senia Pollari, "a sturdy young woman from Finland," as her daughter, Senia Croonquist Hart, remembered her in a speech delivered to the

Yellowstone Corral of Westerners in 1984. Soon after her parents married in 1914, they began "exploring the nearby canyons for a likely place for their dream occupation—that of taking care of 'dudes' who wished to experience the beauty of the high country."

Of the two, young Al knew something of what lay at the core of that dream. He hiked the mountains between Red Lodge and Yellowstone Park throughout his childhood. Today, this area remains largely a wilderness of high mountain ranges, steep and forested river canyons, and broad park-like grasslands that are still home to North America's major wild predators—grizzly bear, grey wolf, and mountain lion. His daughter makes a point that her young father always went into the backcountry "with his parents' permission. The only question they asked was 'which way are you going, Al?'" Such insouciance might strike some today as a criminal form of parental neglect, though we might assume his parents shared popular notions about the backcountry as an ideal place for a young man to learn his own physical and psychological measure. Contemporary adventures by figures such as the Eric Sevareid or William O. Douglas would bear this out: young men were granted a great deal of latitude to test their mettle in wilderness. By the age of nineteen, Al Croonquist had worked as a fishing guide in that vast, rugged territory southwest of Red Lodge.

Whether Senia Pollari fully shared the belief that running a dude ranch was a "dream occupation," we can only wonder. Perhaps she did. After all, she grew up in the shadow of the Beartooth Mountains into which families ventured along primitive roads and trails to fish, hunt, gather, and otherwise recreate. It was also a progressive era when suffragettes demanded not just the vote but equal pay for equal work. A growing sense of confidence and pride were the consequence of newfound liberty. In 1916, Montana elected the first woman to Congress, a progressive Republican, Jeanette Rankin. Men, however, built the camp, and Senia, after whom the camp is named, was the first cook "in the early years when the stove was set in a large canvas tent." This suggests a somewhat less dreamlike arrangement based on well-defined gender roles. The difficult conditions under which she did the cooking are easily imagined.

Once Senia no longer cooked for the work crews or dudes, the hiring of a cook became the topic of a local vaudeville musical comedy, the playbill of which still exists: "*Wanted, a Cook, a musical love story of Camp Senia.*" Or rather, the keeping of a hired cook in the kitchen became a topic of local hilarity. The play takes place, not coincidentally, in late afternoon, by which time dudes would have developed both a powerful appetite and large thirst. The dramatis personae suggests not so much a classless society as one in which different classes are thrown together, perhaps a little awkwardly. Among the characters are Croon Alquist (proprietor), Button (a wrangler), Bobbie Van Bibber (runaway tourist), Mildred Millionbucks (another runaway), Mrs. De Puster Jones Smyth (grass widow), and the apparently volatile Irish cook, Mrs. Bridget O'Flanigan Washington, played ably by Mr. Carl J. Matthews, who didn't get a singing number. The familiar conflict between these stock characters from eastern social classes trying to survive the conditions of their summer holiday in the egalitarian Eden of the West suggest that the frustrations of the tourist service economy had already become fodder for local eye rolling. That the year-round residents of Red Lodge sympathized with the trying conditions under which Senia Pollari and her successors in the kitchen labored reminds us, at least, that this was perhaps a "dream occupation" with stipulations.

Before the young couple could fully realize their dream, however, the First World War intruded. The stigmatic Al was forced to return from his forest reverie to run the family business in Red Lodge, while his twenty-twenty-vision brother served abroad. After the war, the young Croonquists returned to the forest and completed the first building, the main lodge, in 1919. For ten years, until the stock market crash of 1929 and the subsequent Great Depression, the Croonquists catered to a mostly eastern clientele, as many as forty dudes at a time. With a wink of good humor directed at the tony set they hoped would frequent the camp, they called this twenty-five-by-thirty-five-foot log cabin "The Lobby." During the following decade, the Croonquists and their similarly minded friends built eighteen cabins and assorted outbuildings in what is familiar to us today as Western Rustic Style, a rural corollary of Craftsman design then at the height of its popularity.

An early promotional pamphlet, *Away to the West: To a Dude Camp Vacation in the Rocky Mountains*, says, with perhaps too obvious transparency, that dudes would pay "$25.00 a week, $100.00 a month, and $2.00 transportation each way from Red Lodge." Apparently, there was no sliding scale for extended stays. Though the camp thrived, its success proved short-lived. After the crash, "all standing reservations for Camp Senia, where most guests returned year after year, were cancelled for the summer of 1930." Between 1929 and 1938, the camp reincorporated under different business structures, was rented out as a geological base camp over several more summers, and finally was purchased by the Camp Senia Corporation, which persists to this day, maintaining the cabins as summer homes. The camp was added to the National Register of Historic Places in 1988.

⌀

Our guide, as voluble as she was affectless, led the way down the hill along Senia Creek. As a result of the record winter snow pack and a cold, wet, prolonged spring, the creek had overflowed its banks, flooding the gated road that bisects the camp. Debris washed down and rushing water from the creek gouged out the roadbed. Several cabins experienced minor flooding before she and the others managed, in the dark, to redivert the water into the creek.

For the next two hours, she led us from one cabin to the next. The cabins are scattered on both sides of the old Camp Senia Road, which intersects the main West Fork Road below to the east and above the camp to the west. Most of the cabins are clustered along six hundred eighty feet of property between the road and the West Fork of Rock Creek. They are connected by stone-lined paths.

We soon arrived at "The Lobby" at the center of camp, which once served as a gathering area, camp store, and reading room. Though its conventional saddle-notched corner timbering is a familiar characteristic of log cabin design, the Lobby differs from the remainder of the camp in that its walls are constructed entirely of logs; the other cabins are constructed of both cobbles and logs. Below it stands a small building, easily mistaken for the first I saw when I had earlier passed through the camp. The cabin that captivated me for the past decade, though, is no cabin. Rather, it turned out to be one of several coolers scattered about Camp Senia. In a simple but ingenious design, the lower walls of this small rectangular building are constructed of uncoursed native stone, that is, irregular river cobbles. The walls and flooring are built over a small stream that flows into and out of the structure at forty degrees Fahrenheit. The upper walls are screened to enhance air circulation. It is a reliable, simple, one might even say *green* form of refrigeration now commonly used to cool beer. Admittedly, it's a gleeful fact that my first glimpse of the camp, which provoked such a wave of nostalgia that I have ridden it this far, was neither cabin nor playhouse, but the place where they once kept the eggs, milk, and meat to fatten dudes.

Just below the Lobby we crossed on two newly constructed bridges to an island in the creek and to the south shore. On the south side of the creek, we were technically no longer in the historic district. But here on a low hillside above camp were two side-by-side cabins, contemporary with those below, owned by an elderly woman. The cabins, under a sign constructed of fire-salvaged materials and reading "Trail's End," are small and simple, with structural features typical of the rustic style: decorative bracings under the porches and window boxes that incorporate burled tree limbs as an organic accent. What impressed us were the handmade rustic benches, tables, and brooms, all fashioned from materials close at hand. Many other building materials were by necessity carried into the camp from Red Lodge, but in this particular instance, and often throughout the camp, we encountered the aesthetic assumptions of the Arts and Crafts movement and its socialist progenitor William Morris's preference for material of native wood and stone, of simple furniture made in situ, and translated here into a style typical throughout the rural American West and national parks.

According to the National Register of Historic Places's application materials for Camp Senia, the Croonquists hired a "crew of carpenters and masons from Red Lodge who . . . were mostly Finns." The narrative of the cabins' architectural significance goes on, however, to point out that "the buildings don't embody the characteristics of traditional Finnish vernacular architecture," which prefers hewn rather than unhewn logs. Although Finnish and Western Rustic styles share the feature of "saddle-notched corner timbering used at Camp Senia . . . the battering of the sawn log ends" isn't a Finnish style either. It's something more often associated with the American Craftsman style, in which battered foundations (sloping backward and upward from the ground), tapered porch-supports, and pedestals are all common.

Still, it's worth a moment's aside to remember that the Arts and Crafts movement was ubiquitous throughout northern Europe, as well as in Canada and the United States. The nineteenth-century Finnish artist Axel Gallén built Kalela, his rural home and studio that blends Arts and Craft movement values with vernacular Finnish design. The logs of his cabin, which were cut and shaped by rural craftsmen, are hewn. One might, therefore, reasonably assume that the Finnish carpenters working for the Croonquists were no less exposed to the aesthetic assumptions of the Arts and Crafts movement and the expression of its aesthetic assumptions in the construction of nearby national parks. And it's no coincidence that among the members of the Croonquists' building crew was one M. I. Tuttle, who "worked on the crews building a number of log cabins in Yellowstone National Park and Estes Park in Colorado" and who would have been familiar with the popular style that guided the building of these parks. As Linda Flint McClelland points out in her exhaustive study, *Building the National Parks: Historic Landscape Design and Construction*:

> By the 1920s, when National Park Service landscape engineers were working out a program of landscape design for national parks, there existed a well-established philosophy for park design drawn from the practices and precedents in landscape architecture and architecture. . . . These trends merged most emphatically in the Arts and Crafts tradition spurred by California's development of the [Craftsman] bungalow.

During my first visits as a child to national parks, parkways, and national forest campgrounds in the East, this architecture made a lasting impression with its massive, durable, and monumental scale that in effect mirrored America's natural beauty. Thanks to my grandfather, I associated its origins with a time of national crisis during the Great Depression, and because he regaled me with tales of that time, such Craftsman architecture underwritten by the US government came to represent a time of egalitarian values, national accord, and common purpose. That period of his youth lives in my imagination almost as clearly as if I had experienced it myself. And it's precisely the same architecture, on a much more modest scale, that we encounter throughout Camp Senia.

From Trail's End we looked back across the creek at the entire camp. Prominent just above the creek to our right stood the Croonquist's Second Residence. This is a particularly striking cabin and an ultimate expression of the aesthetic assumptions the Croonquists and their associates brought into the forest. The Second Residence was constructed in 1927; that is, at the height of the camp's popularity, two years before the Crash. It looks out at the West Fork of Rock Creek, and across the creek at the rock slides on the north face of the twelve thousand five hundred foot Silver Run Peak. Like most of the other cabins, its construction is of uncoursed native stone and lodgepole pine on the exterior walls. The official description of the cabin reads: "The corner detailing of the stone walls is of particular interest in that the stone protrudes at right angles beneath the butt ends of the logs, extending the angle of the battered log ends to the ground." Two symmetrically placed seven-by-eleven-foot gabled porches extend to the south, perpendicular to the east-west axis of the main gabled roof. One of these shelters a single Dutch door painted a faded shade of bright green. There are burled wood handles on the Dutch door that opens into the kitchen. The other porch is distinguished by twelve-light double doors—extravagant, perhaps, given the rustic qualities of the architecture, but lovely— that allowed us to peer into the living room. Between the gabled porches are two nine-light casement windows. A large exterior native stone chimney dominates the east elevation of the cabin. The overall impression is one of balance and harmony. But the porch with double doors drew the most attention. The exposed logs and bent and burled trim and the handmade rustic settee constructed of bent wood and woven wood fiber represent the interpenetration of the interior and exterior, the made and the natural, the domestic and the wild—one of the aesthetic goals of Arts and Crafts style adopted from traditional Japanese design. It's precisely this achievement that's absent from many Modernist spaces, an absence we've grown so accustomed to, we're not even aware of such harmonies as exist in Camp Senia. The Croonquist's "dream" is a reminder that the soul-deadening, alienating tendencies of contemporary built environments are not fate, but choices.

❦

Camp Senia's purpose, like most ventures in the United States, was to make money, specifically from the tourist trade. Tourism in the American West is so pervasive today that it's simply taken for granted. Most of us don't consider that tourism was an expression of a peculiarly American idealism before it became the garish practice we've grown accustomed to. That the history of the idea is rather more compelling than a crass economic opportunity probably doesn't occur to us at all.

The American encounter with wild nature, from the Transcendentalism of Emerson and Thoreau to the rugged ordeals endured by John Muir and Theodore Roosevelt to the rucksack revolution of Beat Generation dharma bums to the present, promises the idealistic seeker a more robust spiritual and physical health. It's a familiar American trope. In wilderness, we still believe, isn't only the preservation of man, but also a soul's purifying encounter with life uncorrupted by modernity.

Early in the twentieth century, trains brought city dwellers to the West, to Billings for example, and on up to Red Lodge along the spur line, then by horse cart or horseback into the Beartooth Mountains, where they could spend a month in the restorative environs of Camp Senia. Unlike city life with its supposed inauthenticity and dissipations, visitors to Camp Senia would discover that in the Montana wilderness there existed an egalitarian society where, "There Are No Conventionalities . . . Old Clothes and Outing Togs Are the Rule."

Camp Senia's registration as a National Historical District states that if it wasn't the ur-type of western tourist destination, then it was at the very least "the earliest property to be developed in the Beartooth Mountains for the express purpose of operating a dude ranch and fishing camp for tourists." The document points out that tourism of this sort "was a rather novel idea in 1917 when construction began." This is either quaint or ironic, coming well after the fact of the camp's origins, and perhaps it's both; that is, it knowingly voices not only the differences but the similarities between the American West of the Roaring Twenties and our own era, characterized by steroidal "vacation cabins" whose scale is cathedral-like and whose ostentation is pure egotism, a vulgar insult to the beauty of the landscape and evidence of the end of any egalitarian American dream.

The 1920s were certainly characterized by their own excesses, as is our era of boom and bust. But at the risk of expressing nostalgia for the modest scale, intimacy, and aesthetic loveliness of the cabins in Camp Senia, these are qualities of being in the world—modesty, intimacy, loveliness—ubiquitous then but largely foreign to us today. The camp is full of vernacular examples of the same Arts and Crafts movement in architecture and design that reached the height of its popularity and influence at precisely the moment the Croonquists went into the forests along the West Fork of Rock Creek and began building their dream camp. As with the cult of wilderness that developed in the early twentieth century and that Roderick Nash discusses in depth in his seminal *Wilderness and the American Mind*, so with architectural design: Camp Senia isn't so much an ur-type as it's an expression of longing for a timeless, idealistic, spiritual, and humane way of living at domestic ease in nature.

Bachelard seems sympathetic toward our desire "to know our-selves in time, when all we know is a sequence of fixations in the spaces of the being's stability." I wonder, though, is he contrasting two varieties of time and being, and how we might endeavor to reconcile them? We understand our finite selves only too well—our lives fixed within a sequence of events whose horizons are in-ception and death, and perhaps, if we're fortunate, life after death in the memory of others. I don't think Bachelard has in mind here the finitude of self, but spaces that "suspend" time, so that the self doesn't "melt away." Such spaces make it possible for us, despite our finite lives, to experience permanence and continuity in place. In intimate spaces where time suspends, we find depth of presence that resists obliteration. We're a part of that stability of being, not apart from it, and share that awareness with all of life. "In its countless alveoli," Bachelard writes, "space contains compressed time. That is what space is for." I take him to mean that such spaces allow us to breathe the depths of time and feel the fullness of being. That is, in no small way, an expression of the humane ideals of Craftsman design.

That summer when I first visited Camp Senia, I painted the walls of the living and dining rooms of our own little Craftsman bungalow "Italian Rose," as the paint chip read, a color that re-minded us of the sandstone in parts of Arches National Park. We hadn't considered the intimate way the room would glow on win-ter nights, lit by a floor lamp. Nor could we have predicted the ea-gerness with which we would hurry home at dusk to sit and read in that calm, warm room. We realized only later that the color we sought out every evening is perhaps the color of the light that shines in the womb, where human awareness flickers awake.

Bachelard's exuberant claim that "childhood is certainly greater than reality" seems to bear this out. It was, after all, "compressed time" of childhood that I glimpsed in the drive-by with my friend, wakened memories of rooms, even natal memories, that enchanted me long ago, and drew me back inevitably to Camp Senia a decade later. I'd stumbled onto an unlikely portal into the alveoli of the past where I could breathe intimacy.

Also, in the vernacular architecture of Camp Senia there exists a humanely scaled solution to the alienating forces of industrial society that the Arts and Crafts movement and American Craftsman style reacted against. Like Romanticism's reaction to similar stresses over a century earlier, Camp Senia also situates itself in an older idea about nature and its hygienic spiritual qualities, an encounter with which may result, as a prospectus for the camp claimed, in "the literal recreation of any town-wearied member of the Fraternity-of-the-Out-Doors." This may strike us today as half-baked balderdash, though it's still very much the stuff of advertising, amateur poetry, and nature blogs. Nevertheless, in Camp Senia we find ourselves face to face with human "intimacy in immensity," as Bachelard calls it, an aesthetic reverie that continues to assert its progressive and humane prerogatives, emphasizing health, harmony, and happiness, and if not in a classless society, then in one where classes share common ground, a hardy regard and respect for their shared responsibilities and higher purposes. One can only wish.

Later, thinking about that sense of inclusion that our guide offered when we introduced ourselves, I was reminded of the usually unsung final stanza of "This Land Is Your Land," which is probably truer to past and present reality than to reverie: the No Trespassing sign that Woody Guthrie looks on the backside of is blank. That side, the singer declares, is our true inheritance and welcomes us all. Woody Guthrie expresses here the longing, and, because it's largely opposed by the status quo, one of the tensions fundamental to American society. The Craftsman Movement tried to find an all-encompassing aesthetic expression of that same longing. But the concentration of power among feudal-minded state capitalists has long opposed such egalitarian stirrings.

In an op-ed that appeared in the *New York Times* several years ago, Timothy Egan expressed this similar egalitarian pride that used to seem more common in the rural American West than it is today. "Not long after I was old enough to cast my first vote," Egan wrote, and he could just as well have been expressing the experiences of hundreds of thousands of similar young people like myself in the 1970s and before, "I realized that with American citizenship came a birthright to my summer home. . . . We owned it—lake, mountain and forest, meadow, desert and shore. Public land . . . my summer home—which I share with 310 million fellow Americans." Re-reading the entire article today, I feel unaccountably patriotic, teary-eyed even, dreaming of a more egalitarian America I want to believe in more now than ever, as extremists in our political class seem determined to play ideological chicken with national calamity.

The woman who reminded me of all this, our generous guide through Camp Senia, it turned out, was Canadian by birth. She suspected none of what she provoked in the instant she spoke to reassure us of our welcome there in the mountains of south-central Montana.

THE ECLIPSE I CALL FATHER

Fifteen years have passed since, unexpectedly, the eclipse I call my father appeared unbidden during dinner with my almost grown sons. He was even more an occluded presence to them than to me and meeting him was quite a shock for all of us. In some way it must have been inevitable. Something my beloved younger son said didn't sit well with me and simmered all week until dinner that Sunday evening, when he delivered a speech justifying a decision he'd come to that he knew I would not approve. I dismissed his argument as specious. At this point, his older, no less beloved brother defended his younger brother's need for independence, telling me, "You wouldn't know what it's like, all the pressures you put on us—you didn't have a father!"

I was totally undone. Under attack, my psychic household crumbled. I rose from my seat and shrieked, "I have a father! Goddamn you all, I have a father!" Dishes and wine glasses shattered in the kitchen as my rage swept past. Moments later I was sitting on the edge of my bed, my sons on either side of me, holding me in their arms, begging me please to calm down. My head in my hands, I kept sobbing, "But I have a father!"

❧

My first memory of my father is of the two of us driving home from his parents' junkyard in their midnight-blue Coupe DeVille. I stood beside him, holding onto the back of the seat, trying to balance as the seat kept tipping forward. This must have been the autumn of 1961. We were following my mother, piloting her more ordinary, antacid-green 1952 Ford Coupe.

"You want to bump your mother?" he asked.

No one had ever asked me such a question. It seemed at odds with ordinary reality, insofar as I'd mastered the ordinary. Nevertheless, like the child who has yet to touch the hot stove top, I said, "Yes. Let's bump her."

"Hold on," he said as he braked to turn off State Street onto Parkway Boulevard. In that time, long before the invention of car seats for children, safety belts, or seat backs that locked upright, the seat folded forward, tossing me toward the windshield. He grabbed me by the collar of my winter coat and pulled me upright as we veered off Parkway onto West Twenty-Fourth, several blocks from our house. He accelerated, drew close to her, and then slowed as he positioned the Cadillac behind the rear bumper of the Ford.

"Watch," he said and grinned with glee.

He placed the two black rubber tusks that protruded from the grille against the back bumper of the Ford, hit the gas and then quickly braked, nudging my mother hard from behind, and sending me lurching headfirst into the dash. He laughed, delight as much by the slapstick of my tumbling over again as by the way the Ford Coupe lifted and collapsed on its springs. A little chastened and more cautious now, I place my arms around his neck for a more secure handhold and recomposed myself on the seat next to him.

"Do it again," I said.

He did it again. This time, it was my mother's head that hit the steering wheel then whip-lashed from the impact. Success! All the way up Twenty-Fourth Street, and then all the way to our house at the end of Pleasant Place, the walrus-faced Cadillac shoved the lurching Ford.

Once we parked in the gravel driveway and shut off the engines, my mother leaped out of the Ford and erupted in one long, unpunctuated, incoherent harangue of my father. By this point in my life, neither her vocabulary nor the tone of her anger sounded unfamiliar. My father defended himself only with giggles. He never said a word, but we ran around the front yard screaming in mock terror, then turned on my mother and chased her up the driveway, then up the porch stairs, laughing and groping her in the glow of the streetlight as she fumbled the key in the front door. Once inside, he dropped his wool coat on the floor and stripped off his shirt and dungarees. "Come on," he said. "Let's get her!" I stripped, and together we chased her from room to room, upstairs and down to the basement. An ordinary night at 2521 Pleasant Place.

◌

On Saturday afternoons early in the spring of 1962, a woman standing next to me in the group of mothers and children on the grassy runway would tell everybody to—quick!—look up at the sky.

"There," she shouted and pointed her finger.

And then a child's voice: "There. I see them."

For a moment, I could see nothing *there* but the blue of heaven. Then, I saw the bodies of men, our fathers and husbands, who had just tumbled out of the small plane. Soon, three orange tendrils emerged, trailing behind their falling bodies; then their parachutes irised open into orange circles, bright against the dark blue: my father and his comrades sailing toward us who stood on the earth below gaping in wonder.

My father so enjoyed parachuting that he and his friends decided it might prove a better and far more exciting livelihood than working in steel mills or junkyards. They called themselves Skydiving Unlimited: Don Kiggins of Canton, Bill Copper of Maximo, Marvin Axelrod of Alliance, and Jim States of nowhere in particular, as he listed no hometown on the business card. Another friend, Ray Mangus, was their pilot. Their logo consisted of a stylized parachute that looked like a carpenter's inverted plumb bob with wings curving upward from the vertex of the bob's point. In not quite parallel structure, and having the odd rhythm of an arbitrary list, their business card detailed the services they provided patrons: "LICENSED INSTRUCTION in Sport Parachuting—skydiving PARACHUTE Equipment Sales & Rentals EXHIBITION JUMPS PARACHUTES FOR HIRE." You could write to them at 8970 Manchester Road, North Lawrence, Ohio.

So far as I was aware, these ambitions encountered one significant complication.

Good Friday, 1962, my father and mother tossed their luggage in the backseat of the Cessna before flying off for a brief vacation. It was cold and rainy in Ohio, as good a reason as any to leave. They were going to Florida. My only doubts about their intentions revolved around the question of why they weren't taking me along as promised. My grandfather Peters, my mother's father, stood with me on the grassy runway at the airport east of town watching them board the plane. He was a man of peculiar locutions that frustrated me for many years as I struggled to understand him. As my parents settled into their seats in the Cessna, he muttered something I would hear him repeat often in the years to come, as always, deliberately mangling the common wisdom: "Glass people don't throw stone houses." He was always present to witness these leave-takings, and then always willing to take me into his considerate care once the little plane vanished into the cloud canopy. I can't summon a single incident at that airport when either of my father's parents was present. My Grandfather Peters, though, was often there, and as often exchanged grave words with my parents, after which I stayed on the ground with him.

My parents taxied to the head of the runway. My father revved the engine for takeoff, and they began to bounce north along the grassy runway toward the woods and smokestack of the Spam factory. As they reached the velocity of flight, something went wrong, and instead of climbing into the air, which by then seemed to me a routine expectation, the plane abruptly flopped over, its engine cowling and propeller cutting into the sod. We'd no idea if they were injured, and we stood there stunned, a quarter mile away, staring at the wreckage of the upside-down plane and its mangled propeller, as unnatural and awkward-looking as a bug on its back.

"Dear god, no," my grandfather said under his breath, as though afraid to say too loudly what he feared. Then we started running toward the plane.

When we were a few feet shy of the wrinkled fuselage, the doors swung open on each side of the cockpit and like jacks-in-the-box my parents flopped out. My mother seemed shaken, a little wobbly, and silent. My father, though, cocky and boisterous as usual, laughed with the febrile courage of a twenty-two-year-old, rather more exhilarated than intimidated by the casual nearness of injury or death.

They walked back up the runway with us, my father joking with his grim-faced father-in-law and poking me in the ribs, trying to make me giggle.

"Maybe next time we'll make it to Florida," he said. "And little Daver Alan, you'll have to come along."

❧

I can't remember when or how my father's wallet came into my possession. By the time I had outlived him by several decades, I opened that wallet and found a receipt, No. 946, from Alliance

Air Service Flight and Ground School, signed by someone named Clyde and dated the twenty-second of May 1962, just days before my father and his partners' first scheduled exhibition as professional skydivers. My father paid twenty dollars on account that day and left a balance of seventy. The bill is for hanger space rental for the airplane he had just purchased for Skydiving Unlimited to replace the Cessna 172B that he wrecked earlier that spring during a failed takeoff on Good Friday.

I also found and kept a typed memo from the Parachute Club of America, signed by R. A. Gunby:

> Since it is not fair to charge you the complete annual dues
> for only the remainder of 1961, we are starting your member-
> ship as of the date shown on your card. This covers you for
> both the remainder of 1961 and the whole of 1962.

That membership card is lost, but the fair-mindedness of Mr. Gunby remains and fills me with nostalgia for the year 1962, when the value of club membership was something more meaningful than just another opportunity to make an extra few dollars. Clearly, Mr. Gunby was a believer, forward-looking, full of the optimism and good intentions that characterized the era. After all, isn't starting such a new business a sign of moxie and cheerfulness, full faith in the future, a dedication to faithful service? All sunny platitudes, though there was little in the everyday world about which to feel sunny. The events of Memorial Day 1962 would soon predispose our little family to the dread that pervaded the world later that autumn, during the Cuban Missile Crisis. Even that spring, my father's conversations with my mother had become, if not lurid and melodramatic, then certainly prophetic. If he was full of hope about his business future, he never said so to her.

"My number's coming up," he told her that spring, an oddly fatalistic claim for a twenty-three-year-old. He would wake from nightmares screaming that he was in his grave and couldn't stop mourners from throwing dirt in his face.

"Please, promise to take my ashes up to thirty thousand feet," he said to my mother. "Scatter them across the sky."

This hyperbolic request may have expressed the very real concern others had regarding what seemed to be our fast-approaching universal fate, the logical outcome of Cold War anxieties. My father never spoke in metaphors, though, and so his interests were limited to his own, albeit hyperventilating, self-concern.

⌁

I wasn't quite four years old in the spring of 1962, so I can't say with much certainty that I remember any of these events leading up to Memorial Day or after. Whenever I rehearse the past for her, however, my mother stops me and asks, "You really remember that?" In the aftermath of that Memorial Day, did she tell me herself all that I claim to remember? Or did I invent her memory of what she might otherwise have wished to forget? One thing I remember vividly, though, and so does she, is how we often found ourselves trying to discover my father's whereabouts that spring. His peregrinations always led him away from work. We knew not to look for him at the family's junkyard at midafternoon, because he would have left the brothers Crow in charge and departed early.

We might spot him standing in front of the window at Madson's Grille, watching the chicken fat drip from the rotisserie. Or walking our junkyard dogs, Whitney and Antonius, along State Street. Or stopping in for a lime phosphate at Turner Drug & Camera. He might be seated in a booth at Shaffer's Diner or on a swivel stool at the low counter at Heggy's, the air heavy with the smell of roasted nuts and molten chocolate. If all else failed, our search led late in the day to the airport, where we might find him at the north end of the hanger, on one knee, shooting his .22 Browning rimfire rifle at beer bottles that lined a weedy berm of dirt and gravel. Nothing delighted him so much as squeezing the trigger of that semi-automatic—one-two-three-four-five times down the line—and watching in fascination as, a fraction of a second later, the amber bottles burst into little shattered exclamations of shock.

At other times, we might find him folding the orange ripstop nylon parachutes on the concrete floor of the hanger. I always felt a twinge of dread each time he turned from packing the main parachute to the little secondary parachute he wore on his belly.

"In case the main chute fails, I pull this," he said, grasping the ripcord. Parachutes fail? Hence an emergency parachute? This didn't so much reassure me as it conjured the image of free fall, terminal velocity, and panic. How could he trust his presence of mind in such a circumstance as that and remember to pull the auxiliary rip cord? In any event, I must have looked skeptical.

"It's fail-safe," he said. *Fail-safe* was a strategic term much in use then: the point beyond which nuclear bombers couldn't continue to the apocalypse without specially coded orders to do so. No cause for alarm.

~❧

If it was nearing twilight in the spring of 1962, we would find my father, the Marvelous Marvin, at last. He would be sitting in our booth at the airport bar. Our booth was along the back wall under a faux-leaded-glass hanging lamp. He would be nursing a Carling Black Label and smoking a Lucky Strike. That is, if we found him at all. But assuming we did find him, he was inevitably relieved to see us. Apparently, he'd been looking for us all afternoon, too.

"Where in the world have you guys been?" he said one evening as we slid into the booth. Apparently, we were spoilsports. "I thought you guys might have wanted to go flying this afternoon."

My mother tapped out a Salem, lit it, took a deep draw, tilted her head back and blew a dramatic stream of menthol smoke into the air.

"What do you say we fly to Canton and have dinner at Bender's," she said. Bender's was a very old walnut-and-tile restaurant, and close enough to Alliance that it would be a simple matter to dine there and return home early. Also, this being the glory days of my family's junkyard empire, my grandfather would still have had a tab there. "Afterwards, dessert at Taggart's."

"I thought, maybe the Teahouse instead," my father said. This seemed like a congenial idea to me, as the Teahouse, though a little farther away in Akron, served shrimp chips in a basket as an appetizer.

At this point things became complicated, as the options my young parents enjoyed were many. "Why don't we just go on to Cleveland and then to Put-in-Bay and meet Glen? I bet Glen would meet us there with the boat." Or it might have been Michael Mannheim, or a Jim or a Don, there was an endless array of such men with whom my father entertained himself, and who would have dropped whatever they were doing to join us on an overwrought adventure.

At first my mother must have found this form of living large attractive, though soon the extravagance became maddening and she agitated for him to behave like an adult. Agitating, though, did little good in this regard, as my father was too preoccupied with his desires to be even remotely aware that his wife's frustrations might require him to moderate those desires.

He finished his beer and said, "We could always fly to New York and stay with Dou-Dou and Jake."

We went to New York. Or partway. My parents hadn't bothered to tell Dou-Dou and Jake we were on our way, and they weren't pleased to hear from us, calling from a regional airport outside of Philadelphia several hours later. My father wanted to leave me with my cousin Mark while the two young couples went out to a club in the Village. Dou-Dou must have hung up on him. I recall waking in my own bed the next morning, my parents in the kitchen, where my father consumed his usual dozen eggs, pound of bacon (rendered "kosher" by blackening), and half a loaf of sliced rye bread with cream cheese and strawberry jam.

⌖

For many years, I imagined my father as someone easily dismissed. Childlike, spoiled and selfish, thrill-seeking, short-sighted, perhaps even stupid. But then again, this urge to dismiss him was likely provoked by how easily even the casual mention of his name or fate by anyone beside my mother or grandparents could send me into either a murderous rage or, privately, paroxysms of sorrow. He wasn't quite twenty years old when I was born, and he spent the time that remained for him acquiring toys. In the years between 1958 and 1962 he owned outright (or shares of): two airplanes (one, the Cessna, he crashed during takeoff at Easter time), two speedboats (one he crashed into a dock), as well as stock cars and dragsters (which our employee at Axelrod Auto Parts, George Willard, raced on weekends at the Waco Speedway). But I wonder about this certainty with which I dismissed him.

Not long after my birth, my mother says that he regularly brought his black friends to our apartment, unheard of in small town Ohio in the late 1950s, and no doubt this was a source of outrage and anxiety among our uptown neighbors. One night in 1959, under the expert direction of Riley Sheffield and his companions Beanie and Cricket, my parents received proper instruction in dancing the Hand Jive, which my mother, even at eighty, is still more than happy to demonstrate whenever Bo Diddley comes on the radio. Because he does still come on the radio, that Bo Diddley beat remains an instinctive source of our joy.

My father was not flouting decorum just by taking his black friends into his home or taking them flying in the little Cessna; simultaneously, he was trying to start a nudist colony on a farm near Millersburg "for the obvious health benefits of nature." The year I was born, he flunked out of Mount Union college. All of this unfolded during Eisenhower's last term in office and the advent of "the sixties"—a post-war period, that is, of national abeyance, when the beloved son of the first generation born in America found himself back at work in one of the family's two junkyards on Sebring Road. And so there he sat in a filthy shack, five miles outside of town, trying and mostly failing to behave as a normative adult white male of the late 1950s. That shack at least kept him closer to the world he seemed to prefer—LA, aka Lower Alliance, Ohio, the black ghetto, and the greater degree of freedom it permitted at least him, if not its actual residents.

Not that it was necessarily destined to turn out this way. Somewhere along their trail of retreat from Europe, my father's family had strayed far from the milieu of those Axelrods, who were Decemberists, Bolsheviks, and political theorists, so enmeshed in the politics of their times, not only the KGB but the Czars kept files on their activities. The Gordons, my father's mother's family, possessed a direct blood connection to an albeit less radical, but no less prestigious, northern European intelligentsia, among them a few fanatical Zionists. Trying to explain the source of my bookishness, my grandmother liked to recount that at some point (about which she was always a little vague), our near relations from Lithuania had been to yeshiva and then university and, having emigrated safely in advance of the rise of fascism, arrived in Cleveland and Chicago to assume administrative and academic positions in public schools or private universities. It was possible.

My father and his sister, however, seemed to inherit a passion for the more conventional forms of prestige: access to money. Or more precisely: money and the status that the fabulous overspending of it supposedly bestows. Hence, there was a hyperbolic crassness about us, perfectly expressed by our Cadillacs (or Olds Ninety-Eights after the glory days ended), gaudy jewelry, glitzy steak houses, high-stakes gambling, private planes, speedboats, and weeks in New York every fall to buy the season's new fashions. America, after all, promised the pursuit of unalloyed happiness and the dreck we filled our lives with was evidence of what made us so happy.

Regardless of how I perceived things, my mother, finding herself in the presence of such reverence for my father, bowed to what at least seemed to be the popular sentiment and forgave him within moments of any offense. Even one instance of sexual straying.

"He was just so much damn fun to be around," she said many times, especially when we weren't really having much fun anymore. "I always forgave him everything." As for that instance of infidelity: my mother threatened to kill him. Knowing my mother, I assure you that was no idle threat.

⌖

We spent so much time at the little airport on Route 62 across from the drive-in theater that I thought the hanger and airstrip belonged to us. On weekends the children of Skydiving Unlimited played in the pea gravel while the men worked on engines, spoke "airport talk," and our mothers squealed with feminine admiration. It was here that we learned not only the vocabulary but also the proper rhythm for swearing to maximum effect, as the men who worked in the shadowy hanger behind us, each of them dressed in dungarees and white T-shirts (packages of Lucky Strikes rolled up in their left sleeves), were advanced protégés of Marlon Brando and James Dean.

The delightful scandal of our fathers' vulgarity aside, we children were otherwise preoccupied, sitting where the shadow of the hanger met the summer daylight in an angular slash across the pea gravel and grass runway. We stared across the grassy runway toward Oyster's Dairy, surrounded by fields of tall corn that the Oysters soon would chop for silage.

Across Route 62 from the airport, the drive-in theater, lit up by acres of neon tubing at twilight, was a carnival of lurid colors. The Mahoning Drive-in was the site of my father's legendary attack from the air, Kamikaze-style, as the groping young couples of Alliance looked on in wonder. The advertisements began rolling at dusk, and naturally, Axelrod Auto Parts had purchased one such ad. The soundtrack—a brass fanfare for common men—blared in the speakers hanging on the windows of the cars parked below. The music easily could have accompanied legions of Hollywood light brigades charging on horseback toward each other across the San Fernando Valley.

As the brass fanfare played, gray lines of text appeared, one letter at a time, from left to right, *almost* synchronous with the dramatic voice-over: "At Axelrod Auto Parts our highly skilled staff aims to satisfy all your automotive needs selecting from our extensive stock of high-quality merchandise—Axelrod Auto Parts! Your home for new, used, and factory re-conditioned auto parts! Located just off..." There was something clear-minded about that moment my father turned on the landing lights and flew directly at the five-story screen as though he intended to hit it head-on. His mock aerial attack on the screen ended as he pulled us up at the very last moment, the landing gear just clearing the rim of the screen. He reached for the control panel and the landing lights flicked off as we disappeared into the dark sky.

Daylight transformed the drive-in from a factory of terrors and inconceivable dangers into a dull off-yellow slab of concrete and picket fences. Nevertheless, the older children among us kept us on edge by reading aloud the marquee, advertising the current Buckets of Blood triple-feature that entertained our gleeful parents throughout summer nights. If my companions found those movies disconcerting, our parents regarded them with bravado. And though all of us children would have slept safely in the ample backseats of our parents' behemoth automobiles as the third reel

exhausted itself in the sky above, we spent a portion of those afternoons imagining the mayhem that would progress across the
five-story screen once dusk settled into dark.

"Get that off your head. This is the really good part. You don't
want to miss it," my mother said one night, jerking away the jacket that I wore like a hood over my head. There in the sky above
us the partly burnt and otherwise vivisected face of the monster
in question stared at me. When I shrieked in despair, I only provoked my parents' glee.

Most often, though, we just sat there, the bunch of us, bored in
the open-ended time of childhood, throwing stones at the grass
runway. Then the men dragged the planes out of the hanger, the
necessary repairs made, and confident of their skills as mechan-
ics, we went flying with the members of Skydiving Unlimited.

⁖

Of the many times I recall flying with my father, the most vivid
memory probably never happened. It's indicative of the tenor
of the family romance. I was seated beside my father, my own
controls just out of reach in front of me, so I could mime what
my father was doing as he piloted the plane toward the airport.
We banked west and then south, turning in a wide circle to the
east, heading toward the drive-in across the highway from the
airport. Then we flew up into the low deck of clouds. It grew very
dark for a moment, except for just above the plane, where the
clouds began to thin. The light at the edge of the clouds above
our heads was suffused by water vapor and gave the surfaces of
the wings and our faces a pale golden glow. We came abruptly
to the edge of the clouds, passed through a wisp, and directly
before us stood the cliff face of the abandoned clay mines behind
the College Plaza (America's first strip mall). We were off course,
a mile and a half west of the airport. The cliffs were yellowish
and covered with scrub. The abandoned brickyards were nearby,
across Mahoning Avenue.

Terrified to see the clay mines ahead of me, I reached forward and pulled back hard on the controls. The plane shot straight up into the air as we cleared the cliff and the scrubby sumac and blackberry briars that lined its rim. My father laughed, congratulating me on my good sense and instinct for self-preservation. In a recurring nightmare, I find myself on the ground below those cliffs, the earth more like carved human flesh than mined clay, and the paths that lead from one open pit to another wind past ponds of acid and toxic fog.

⌀

Skydiving Unlimited contracted for its first exhibition at a small airport just outside of Massillon, Ohio, on Memorial Day, 1962. It was in every sense an ordinary late spring day in Ohio. Warm, sunny, becoming muggy as the morning wore on, still early enough in the year that the entire landscape erupted with a deep, plush exuberant green. My father flew to Massillon with his partners, but my mother took me with her in the Cadillac to make a proper impression about the quality of the men (and their families) providing this form of highly professional, dangerous entertainment. My mother and I intended to watch the festivities throughout the day, but we weren't going to witness my father and his friends jump later in the afternoon, as it conflicted with my nap.

At some point, I wandered off among a maze of carnival concessionaires and flea market tables. Soon, I was searching for my mother back near the hangers. She had disappeared.

"Your mother's gone up with the men," States' girlfriend Iva told me. Iva was soon distracted, and I jumped down, wiped my face on the shoulders of my T-shirt, and continued to beat about the spectator area, trying to seem confident with my freedom, but feeling nevertheless peevish because of it. Having corralled her own passel of boys, Kiggin's wife caught up with me and hauled me back to the fifty-five-gallon barrel top, which must have marked the agreed-to spot to plant me.

She pointed to the plane passing at that moment right above our heads. "Your mom's up there," she said. "Just sit tight, will you?"

We watched the plane putter over our heads to the south and we craned our necks to watch. Then the plane banked in the air just above the two parallel rows of hangers and the grassy runway between. Overhead again, the plane disappeared over the near ridge of low hills.

And that's it. I remember nothing else of my father's professional debut.

Reunited, my mother and I drove back to Alliance in the late afternoon where she dropped me at my grandparents' house for my nap. She planned to meet my father later for some nighttime boating on Berlin Reservoir. At the left margin of that nap it was still very much daylight, the humidity oppressive, sky beginning to darken with thunderheads. I went to sleep hot and sticky with sweat. When I woke in early evening, though, the air felt cooler, and gusts of wind billowed the curtains in my room. Getting out of bed, I walked to the front door and out onto the elevated concrete pad of the porch; the air was less oppressive than earlier, but a storm threatening.

In Ohio before a storm, the light becomes oddly greenish as the storm prepares to burst. There was always great drama at this moment. Alliance, I was always reassured, is situated on a high point relative to the surrounding countryside, Mount Union, and so there was seldom threat of tornados. Still, the storms rushed in low and it seemed to me that we experienced storms as though from within the roiling storm clouds themselves. Instead of long branches of lightning erupting across the sky, the strikes were instantaneous blasts of light, followed immediately by the inconceivably deep bass rumble of thunder tearing the air apart around us. I often stood on that concrete pad outside my grandparents' house transfixed until someone grabbed me and jerked me inside the door.

My mother describes that evening differently: the air turned deeply violet at the point when it wasn't quite dark yet, and the metallic paint of the stop sign near my parents' house glowed intensely silvery-red, as though lit by a presence within. We recall different twilights. The fundamentals in our lives had shifted. An absence already occupied our private world.

My grandmother was on the phone speaking to my mother and was unaware that I had wakened, gone outside, returned to the house, and was standing in the dusky kitchen just behind her, listening as the storm winds hissed through the window screens. She sat on the stool and leaned against the counter on her left elbow, the black receiver pinched between her left shoulder and ear.

I could vaguely make out my mother's voice, the tone clear and familiar enough. She complained about how my father was late, as he was always late, and was no doubt about to miss yet another rendezvous.

"I don't know how much more I can take," she said to her mother, meaning that Marvin's inability to be where he said he would be at such and such a time had pushed the limits of her patience again. It was an old complaint, one her mother had heard before. Soon enough, my father would turn up at the house on Pleasant Place, and all would be well again. The thunderheads would burst, the sky clear, and they would go boating as planned, a melon-colored moon rising over the lake.

The operator broke in to connect a doctor at the hospital in Massillon. I could hear my mother yelping through the line.

"Good Lord," my grandmother said. "Good Lord, no," as though she could stamp her foot and humiliate bad news, change it to better.

There had been an accident.

A plane crash.

My father was dead.

In an absurdity appropriate to the moment, my mother was standing in the basement of our house on Pleasant Place, trying to shimmy into a skin-tight seersucker dress that tangled around her calves and knees. When the call was interrupted by the doctor, she lost her balance and tripped over my tricycle. I'd left the tricycle in the driveway earlier in the week and my father had backed over it with the Cadillac. An exposed metal edge of that tricycle gouged my mother's knee so that when she arrived at the hospital an hour later, all of her exposed leg was covered in rivulets of dried blood.

My mother's father hurried across town in the rain to fetch his daughter to the hospital in Massillon. My grandfather Peters was one of the few, if not the only, member of our immediate family to treat my mother in a consistently kind manner throughout this time and after. He also had loved my father with the same indulgence as all the others. A former altar boy, my mother's father was, momentary lapses aside, a man with a conscience. He sat there beside her in the front seat of his huge green Hudson, suffering from his knowledge that the unconditional love he felt for his feckless son-in-law ultimately had been a betrayal of his daughter. He had played his own role in this catastrophe.

"And you know, Dauber," he explained years later, addressing me in one of the half-dozen nicknames he called me, "everyone was at fault." So even in death, my father was able to dodge responsibility because no one individual had ever uttered a sobering "*no*" to all the hijinks he pursued without a thought of consequences. That night, however, my grandfather Peters made no effort to explain or excuse anything. "You've never been permitted to live a very happy life," was all he said to his daughter.

No indeed. She wasn't permitted a reprieve. We knew nothing

except for the incontrovertible fact of his death. As none of us had witnessed the accident, and those who survived it had little recollection of what actually occurred, we had to reconstruct the incident from newspaper reports based on interviews with eye-witnesses. For years I tried to convince myself that I witnessed the crash. But that was a dramatic fantasy a child tells. Or perhaps this false witness expressed a desire to return and intervene.

☙

The plane that crashed was a Stimson V-77 Gullwing, recently purchased. My father flew it home from Louisiana to replace the wreckage he made of his Cessna. It was a good deal larger than its predecessor. He and his partners had removed the plush seats to allow the pilot and four jumpers in full gear room enough to pile in. The V-77 was a classic already among those who loved elegantly designed small planes. It had luxurious blue velvet seats, felt ceiling, and mahogany door and panel trim. Its lines were sensuously full and curving, unlike the minimalist lines of a Cessna. The engine cowling in front was open so that you could see the magnificent Lycoming 680-13 through the blur of the wooden propeller.

They had flown that plane all day without incident, much less any hint of mechanical trouble. After taxiing for takeoff and rising several hundred feet in the air, everything seemed ordinary in the extreme. The plane continued to climb slowly, but then it stalled, and instead of gliding on its ample gull wings safely back to earth, it turned nose down and fell straight into the hillside, where it exploded into flames.

"It happened so fast," eyewitnesses said. "There was really nothing we could do."

And yet Cooper, States, and Dick Mangus, the loner who often piloted the plane for them, survived the crash. Though he suffered broken legs and burns over much of his body, Cooper dragged States to safety. He then returned and pulled the unconscious Mangus from the wreckage. After saving Mangus's life, when he realized that his other comrades were unable to free themselves, Cooper attempted yet another act at heroism, returning to the plane. This last effort, however, proved futile, as the heat of the fire drove him back to a safer distance, where he lay down next to States, the two of them alternately groaning and sobbing in pain. This went on for many hours; my mother claims that she will never forget that sorrowful sound when she arrived at the hospital in Massillon. My father and Kiggins, however, weren't so lucky as to find themselves in that shockingly deep, cool grass of an Ohio hillside, much less agonizingly alive in the hospital hours later.

"Your husband and Mr. Kiggins," the doctor said, to lessen the horror of such a death, "died instantly on impact." Their bodies had been tidily incinerated by the subsequent fire. The only thing left to identify my father was his teeth.

~&~

As I looked at the newspaper's front page on Monday evening, our house was very quiet in my father's sudden absence. Although I wish more than ever today that people had come to us, had crowded into our house, had fed us and tried to comfort us, the fact is that no one rushed to my mother's side. Nor did anyone sit *shiva* with us, as my mother was "not really Jewish," as my Jewish relatives liked to say, and besides, my grandmother Axelrod had already mourned four years earlier when my father, in his momentary madness, married a *schixa*. Maybe the Axelrods did sit *shiva* a second time and we were excluded from it? Our exclusion seems likely, as it was generally felt that these events were the just punishment for living outrageously, that we'd gotten our proper desserts; that is, my mother and I were fully beyond the expression of others' sorrow for us.

I sat alone in the living room on the sleek blue Danish sofa, looking at the newspaper, at my father's high school graduation photo next to the photo of Kiggins in his Marine dress blues. Above them there was another, larger photo, taken at dusk with a flash bulb, of the burnt-out wreckage of the plane. All that remained was the metal airframe, every inch of its Ceconite skin melted away by the heat of the fire. I couldn't read, and yet I was aware of exactly what the bold capitalized headlines meant.

Clippings of that article, which my grandfather Axelrod examined obsessively, reappear every so often, though I have always refused to read it, knowing that I would find my own name there. One glance at its layout, the heavy ink, the yellowed newsprint, and that lurid *True Confessions*-style presentation, and I feel suddenly at the mercy of an old and crushing despair. Whenever that article reappears from an old file folder or a relative's dresser drawer, I feel nauseated. Those pictures of their faces and of the wreckage of the plane represent what may be the most intimate and humiliating moment of my mother's and my life, made a matter of public scrutiny.

If my mother was denied the comfort of others in the aftermath of the accident, the formal protocols for a Jewish funeral nevertheless ran their usual course. My father's family buried his remains quickly, in the family plot, where they all lie together now. My mother does not remember my being present at the funeral, but her son was very much present if not accounted for.

I didn't look at the casket, nor did I look at the yellow hole in the earth we lowered him into. No one placed a shovel in my hands so that I could drop the ritual first spade of dirt onto my father's box, as they felt I was still far too young to face such an additional trauma. My cousin held out the spade toward me, but the others shook their heads no. I remained at the periphery of all of this, staring emphatically at my feet, paying focused attention to my left foot, which tapped with maniacal impatience against the cover plate of a water valve. I looked up only three times.

Once, to glance at the black veils and weeping women around me, all of them clothed in stylish black funerary dresses, my great aunts and second cousins, the huge extended family mostly from New York City and Cleveland, and from whose presence I have ever since absented myself.

Another time, I looked up into the limbs of the nearby sycamore tree, where I saw a brilliant red-crested cardinal with whom I played a game of peek-a-boo, but who then darted away.

And a third time, as a small plane flew low above us, causing little hunchbacked, club-footed Rabbi Goran and the entire funeral cortege to pause and look up aghast, confused by whether they should give in completely to despair or laugh aloud at the inexhaustible absurdity and impertinence of life, even in its moment of vanishing.

BOXING LESSONS

"You couldn't beat your way out of a paper sack." That's what my maternal grandfather said as he crossed his arms, shook his head, and sighed with disappointment. My miserable state of existence seemed unmistakable: "You lack the killer instinct."

And why this assessment? I'd come home in a panic from State Street Junior High School after my first day in the seventh grade. Robbie Thompson and his ally Turtle Young had promised "to hurt me good." Why they singled me out, backing me into a corner of the hallway below the cafeteria, where they made their threats, I couldn't say. Their loathing for me, however, seemed universally known, and word of it came to me early that first day.

The one boy, Robbie, the older of the two, who wished to hurt me the most "was adopted"—a resonant phrase, owing to its Dickensian subtext, though Robbie was the son of a banker and lived in a swankier neighborhood uphill from ours. Even so, his being adopted meant that his own status was, to a degree, more contingent than mine. My father had been dead eight years and my mother was living in exile in the next town, so my maternal grandparents housed and fed me six days a week; Tuesdays were reserved for the ministrations of my father's parents. My origins and rearing were a matter of public knowledge, Robbie's perhaps less so. His was a charity case.

To our way of thinking, there was nothing worse than being adopted. Not because of the adoption, but because of the damage that preceded it. The orphanage, the Fairmont Children's Home, still operated south of town and in our imaginations was a circus of pathologies. Whenever we passed the old brick dormitories and surrounding farm fields, an adult warned against the consequence of such events as might lead to our servitude at the Children's Home. "Settle down now or we'll leave you at The Home" was a common threat issued from the front seat. The conditions inside The Home were notoriously awful, we knew, because of the story that accompanied the warning: the orphans had lynched the depraved headmaster in 1944.

That Robbie was saved from the orphanage by a secure upper-middle-class family in no way changed the fact that he was a cruel, one-eyed son of a bitch. Yes, one-eyed. He had a glass eye that stared straight ahead, unblinking, even as he cast a cunning sideways glance at the world with his good eye. Turtle, whose origins he wore like a tattoo, evident even in the snarling expression of his face, came from the rougher, transient neighborhoods just uphill from the black ghetto and the mills. Initiated into the sectarian gang led by Robbie, the Brotherhood, Turtle tagged along to witness his leader's threat. Whereas Robbie was well dressed and neat in preppy, button-down, oxford cloth fashion, Turtle was dirty and badly dressed in an old T-shirt and soiled jeans, with wavy hair that fell to the shoulders of his Army Surplus fatigue jacket. He was missing a front tooth. After Robbie sucker punched me and issued his threat, Turtle grabbed my open shirt collar, pressed me against the brick wall, knee in my crotch, and stared silently into my face. After a long pause, he said: "I'm gonna run race tracks round your eyes."

I nodded, convinced he could and likely would do just that. Then he released me with a shove and followed Robbie down the stairs into the dungeons deep under the school.

My grandfather's intention that evening, as he led the way down into the dank, paneled room in his basement that smelled of sewer gas, was to save my skin. He produced a pair of moldy leather boxing gloves. These gloves, remnants of a time in his own childhood when fisticuffs was still a proper and necessary sport for healthy young boys to excel at, had never appeared before. He laced these around my skinny wrists to demonstrate.

At five feet ten and 225 pounds, his gut notwithstanding, he was a powerfully built fellow whose hirsute body was laced with muscles such as were common when men still did physical labor, a different look than the sculpted appearance of today's protein drink and gym mirror Adonises. "Crouch low," he said. "Keep your elbows close to guard your ribs. Lead with your left, counter-punch with your right. Never roundhouse. Try."

I tried, swinging wide with my right hand. He stepped close, led with his left, and tapped me in the face as I stood there dumb-founded, the boxing gloves now hanging at my sides.

"You can't leave yourself open like that," he warned, stepping back and straightening up to discuss this point. "And remember this, too: under no circumstance should you sucker-punch." This was utterly worthless, he explained, unless one was strong enough to smash the sternum of one's opponent; it would only piss them off. "Dauber," he informed me, using his then-preferred pet name, "you are not that strong. Instead, you might aim for the nose and throat."

Now, he was back in a boxing stance and moving in on me. "When you jab with your left—Dauber, listen to me—always twist your fist to cut flesh. Jab," he said. He flicked the smelly gloves at my cheekbones, then commanded me to "Jab, jab, jab."

He chose this moment to sketch his own history as a pugilist. These tales may have been based, at least in their essential elements, on outright lies. He insisted that he had once been a great brawler. "I knew how to use my hands," he said. He never bullied anyone, but was modest, polite, a perfect little altar boy, ecumenically feared by Catholic, Jew, and Protestant alike because, as he said, expecting me to be quick with an historical allusion, "I walked softly, but carried a big stick." He allowed, though, that he once lost a fight, "took a dive" for his beloved brother, Norm, with whom he quarreled over Norm's unfaithful wife. When challenged by Norm, who later fell apart because of said faithlessness, my grandfather permitted himself to take a beating rather than raise a hand against his own brother. "Am I not my brother's keeper?" he asked as we sparred. I had no idea.

Probably my grandfather wasn't a fighter, but rather more like the fruitcake he seemed, a grown man intoxicated by the comedy of his words. A lapsed Catholic, he enjoyed singing in the high style of the priesthood, gleefully quoting chapter and verse from his Good Book—a mishmash of early twentieth-century immigrant noises from working-class Alliance, Ohio: "Num sareta voita frenyso, chefatche pina mo. Peewee wankum zooy. Dushwuckdas do, yuckish mickafivish, mactavish, sanova beach dundee." This sentence, or any variation on it that may have included as well the noun *fistairus* or pronoun *Swinus Americanus*, he spoke in all contexts, its meaning immediately self-evident.

"Dragoneer," he would say, addressing me in another of his pet names—George, John Funk, Axeldragon (or Axle Draggin'?), Dobido, etc.—"Make with the chafatche. Dushwuckdas do!" He danced around and stomped his feet like Rumpelstiltskin until I acted according to his desire, say, by picking up a drill bit from the workshop table and handing it to him.

For years I imagined myself on the brink of receiving a horse for my birthday, whenever we stopped near a field or wood lot

and he announced, "I'm going to go see a man about a horse now."
Or, in a similar vein, whenever I farted: "Get a shingle and scrape
your leg."

Was it any wonder his pugilistic instructions did me little good
in a street fight? Robbie and Turtle terrorized me with fists that
combined the frightening qualities of quickness and concrete.
They wasted no time thumping me after school that autumn, as I
bobbed, elbows guarding my ribs, a first-class boob, assuming the
proper stance to "jab, jab, jab."

⌖

Late on Saturday afternoons throughout the 1960s, before
I began working at the junkyard of my paternal grandparents,
boxing lessons of another kind arrived via *Wide World of Sports*.
First, one waited through the typical afternoon fare of monster
shows with iconic hosts—Ghoulardi on Channel 8 out of Cleveland, and, decidedly lower budget, The Cool Ghoul on UHF 13
out of Canton. Later at night, depending on the atmospheric
conditions and the ability of the TV's rabbit ears to bring in the
signal, one could tune in to the *Hoolihan and Big Chuck Show*
also on Channel 8 or Chilly Billy's *Chiller Theater* on Steel City
2. Day or night, the monster shows were a satisfying aspect of
each weekend. Being a child during a time of war, I set up an
elaborate machine-gun bunker at one end of the basement opposite the TV and thus was able to protect myself and a grateful
nation from an endless variety of oversized reptiles, the giant
collective id from *Forbidden Planet*, to say nothing of Japanese
actors dressed in baggy "tights" and wearing prosthetic penis-
es for noses. Here was an entire adolescent imagination full of
worthy monsters to slaughter as they attempted to exit the TV
screen and approach across the concrete floor. Assisting in my
patriotic duties were the hosts of the shows, who, at the moment
of climactic violence, appeared superimposed upon the screen

and singing parodies of popular songs, such as "Papa-Oom-Mow-Mow." Which was my cue to open fire.

Even so, I spent dreary Ohio Saturdays awaiting the first notes of the brass fanfare, the voiced-over "Shill of bigotry and the agony of my feet," the appearance of the baggy-eyed, hang-dog stare of Howard Cosell and his hyperbolic introduction of my hero Cassius Clay. A manly Little Richard, Cassius Clay would be hyping his next fight, declaring, "I'm young, I'm handsome, I'm fast on my feet, I can't be beat!" Cassius Clay, who was mocked and abused; Cassius Clay, with whom I fell in love; Cassius Clay, whose joking and dancing play defined for me how arrogance, beauty, and courage are the indivisible, childlike elements of genius only fools dare to despise. Listening to him rhyme, who could doubt that he would win the fight? All he had to do was simply throw a few quick punches during the middle rounds. He spent the early rounds enacting a farce. His arms waving high in the air, he mugged, dodged, and fled wide-eyed in mock terror, until his opponent, appalled by how Clay betrayed conventions, was KO'd as much by confusion as the sudden flurry of left jabs and one deceptive, crushing right hook.

Fighters denounced him, called Clay hateful to everything American, a freak, a clown, "irritatingly confident," a pretty face that needed "butchering." But no one could touch him. Not Sheriff Tuney Hunsaker, not Alonzo Johnson or Floyd Patterson, not Sugar Ray Robinson or Zora Foley, not even the terrifying, renowned thug, Sonny Liston, who was last seen flat on his back after calling Cassius Clay "a faggot." That's an iconic image: Cassius Clay standing over Liston, going berserk, shrieking, "Get up and fight, sucker!"

Clay was no doubt the greatest, "the double-damn greatest," one might say. And more. Much more. What I'm about to repeat is probably a lie, a story from that time still well before Muhammad Ali's rehabilitation as the embodiment of self-congratulatory good intentions toward racial progress. It's a lie about Cassius Clay before he turned professional, a young boxer just returned triumphant from Greece but dejected and in despair because of his nation's racism. He stands down by the Ohio River shore, ready to throw away his Olympic medal, let his gold sink as quickly from sight as any black man might vanish in America, consumed by what preys upon him. It's a lie, a goddamn lie; or if it's the truth, it's a wound as old as our country's original sin.

Either way, a treacherous river flows at the center of it, a river drifted deep with toxic shoals, a river across which slaves who knew they were slaves swam to freedom, if they didn't first drown.

❧

As everyone knows who has read through the lead-footed authorized biography of Muhammad Ali, there is one astonishing passage in the book sure to capture attention. It wasn't written by the biographer, but is quoted from a sports journalist, Jimmy Cannon. The column it's drawn from first appeared in the venerable New York *Daily News* and is offered here as a tactless, clearly nonacademic, tertiary source:

> Clay is a part of the Beatle movement. He fits in with the famous singers no one can hear, and punks who ride motorcycles with iron crosses pinned to leather jackets, and Batman, and the boys with long dirty hair, and girls with the unwashed look, and college kids dancing naked at secret proms held in apartments, and the revolt of students who get a check from dad the first of every month, and painters who copy the label from soup cans, and surf bums who refuse to work, and the whole pampered, style-making cult of the bored young.

Cannon must have been having a good time writing that. He wasn't serious (was he?), because the world he describes with apparent contempt is thoroughly benign. Is it reasonable to suspect poor Jimmy Cannon of a bit of longing for what he missed out on, namely, dancing naked at secret proms held in apartments, or that far more exotic and dangerous dance floor at The Factory? *Andy: call me, please!*

The idea that Cassius Clay was somehow, even in a subterranean way, connected to any of this is ridiculous. Really Cannon *is* missing the point. And probably deliberately. My pugilist grandfather ignored Batman and forgave the Beatles for being whatever they were in his mind, admitting that, "'Hey Jude' might last." Cassius Clay, however, never enjoyed such absolution in our household. And that is because, as Cannon used him in his catalog, *Cassius Clay* was code meant entirely for the consumption of working-class white men, for whom he signified their dismay at the cultural ascendancy of Black Pride.

When Cassius Clay claimed in public he had "no quarrel with them Viet Cong," it was the first time I heard him called Muhammad Ali.

My grandfather was apoplectic. Ali was an unpatriotic abomination. This sudden appeal to pathos was something new and strange. It made me very suspicious of patriotism, as it seemed to be the rhetorical field onto which my grandfather retreated when decency failed. Otherwise, he was anything but a patriot. Once, for instance, when asked what brave deeds he accomplished in the Second World War, he said he served "a proud tour of duty in the Salvation Army." That is, my maternal grandfather, a unionist and a Roosevelt Democrat and an otherwise self-ironic man, when he first heard the name Muhammad Ali, crossed his arms and in a tone of heavily hyphenated invective, pretty much came unhinged. "His name's Clay. And he's a yellow-bellied, draft-dodging, son-of-a-bitching communist."

From that point everything seemed to go wrong. Wars, race riots, coups, assassinations. In 1966, I was eight years old and had no clue about Vietnam or the draft, much less about the Nation of Islam or the Civil Rights Movement. But we all understood even then that Ali's defiance, like the defiant image of Malcolm X that held my attention on the cover of his autobiography, betrayed an old silence about what we feared lay at the foundations of our country. Ali, no less then as President Obama today, challenged that old silence and thus threatened our belief in the most restrictive notions of exceptionalism. White men were as determined then to "take back their country" as the Tea Party or alt-right today. Ali—who never played the Tom nor sucked up, but worshipped Allah, a foreign God, who followed the teachings of Elijah Muhammad and learned to "walk the way of free men," who remained autonomous and apparently refused even the rich white women who offered visits to the Big House for pussy—Ali declined to compromise the way the rest of us do. He refused to drink the poisoned water of that familiar river of self-hatred, and long before it became the fashion, declined to fight in the racists' war.

Before they stripped Ali of his title, before he lost his boxing license, he entered the ring one last time against Ernie Terrel. I watched the fight in the filthy, crowded back room at the house of my friend, Gary Mann. Howard Cosell had made a big deal of how Terrel refused to address Ali by his Muslim name, and so as the fight progressed (though one might say it deteriorated) Ali baited him, called Terrel "Uncle Tom," pummeled him all around the ring, shrieking, round after round, "What's my name?" until Terrel began to convulse and flinch before feinted blows. Ali shouted himself hoarse—"What's my name?"—as if Ernie Terrel, no differently than my oddly patriotic grandfather, had the slightest idea why he wouldn't form those five dangerous syllables on his own American tongue.

᪣

There was wealth in our town, but it held itself apart, uphill from the houses of labor, in the neighborhoods where my nemesis, Robbie Thompson, lay his head nightly on a feather pillow. The city below arranged itself as an amphitheater, or a cutaway of Dante's *Inferno*, each neighborhood divided along ethnic and racial lines, each neighborhood forming one more semi-circle of Hell: in the outermost were the wide, tidy streets and "naturalized" forest lawns of the professional class of respectable Catholics, Protestants, and a half-dozen elderly Jews, then German, Irish, and Italian Catholics, descending downhill to grimy slums of eastern European Catholics, and then the inner rings, nearest the factories, in perpetual stink of industry: the ruins of the black ghetto. At the dead center of which stood my paternal grandparents' junkyard: Axelrod Auto Parts.

Every one of us knew his true identity, and it was a lot closer to Ernie Terrel's perspective than Ali's. And we knew that our school (the one to which we stayed true in 1971) was our equivalent of the factories where we planned to matriculate as hod carriers. That is, at school, we assembled, uncomfortably removed from our neighborhoods, gathered around long tables face to face at lunchtime, passionately arguing about Muhammad Ali, who had returned unvanquished from exile.

There was no way for us to judge the change four years had made in him, nor how, in some way, it would happen to each of us. Even Ali, once the most beautiful man alive, had grown slower, puffy-faced, unable to dance for hours on his toes. Nevertheless, his boast that he could still "float like a butterfly and sting like a bee" remained what our white fathers feared and therefore despised in free-minded black men, and what the black sons who shared that table with us longed for in their own fathers. Having experienced their own moment of outrage at the river's shore, their fathers had learned to become conveniently invisible, to keep quiet after surviving past their twentieth birthdays. These men were allowed only to perform an obligatory, comic display of joy—perhaps a little celebratory dance—when their own sons earned their allowance of life's acclaim on the track oval, basketball court, or gridiron, before they were smothered by what Ira Johnson, one of my older teammates on the basketball team, called "the simple facts be facts, fool."

Quiet and shy as they were in the classroom, there always flared in those young men an articulate rage that verged on self-immolating joy whenever they described Ali's return to the ring after three long years of banishment for criminal lack of patriotism toward his racist nation. They regarded his return as an event of historic proportion. Never mind that he returned merely to box a journeyman like Jerry Quarry, who was happy just to be slaughtered by Ali, or stout Oscar Bonavena, the Argentine Bull, who stood in the ring, mouth gaping, just another dumbass destined to die in a Nevada whorehouse. These skinny black sons of almost invisible fathers leaped from folding chairs to demonstrate the Ali shuffle and, a few years later, rope-a-dope, recited his couplets as though reciting catechisms, playing the dozens, embellishing his lines with poetry of their own. We laughed throughout the entire lunch hour. "Listen, you ratchet-nose motherfucker, if my man don't take Frazier down in three, I'm going to leave this town in *your* daddy's LTD!"

Frankie Everett's father, however, had been on *Candid Camera*. He was a traffic cop, and a famous one, and for a time the exception to the rule of invisibility. There was a circle painted on the asphalt at the center of the intersection of State Street and Union Avenue, where, periodically, the police would turn off the traffic light and Frankie's father would dance. To say he directed traffic would be like saying that Thelonious Monk played a keyboard. Frankie's very dark father would pull on fine white gloves and proceed to spontaneously interact with the chaos of approaching traffic in such a way as to render it a work of art. There, at the center of the busy intersection, surrounded by the fumes of leviathan-like Chryslers, Chevys, and Fords, was a point of human calm and grace, albeit a decidedly funky grace. If a motorist from out of town didn't know what to expect, that motorist would gape in astonishment at the human perfection of movement that danced before him. For those of us familiar with his presence, we took him a little too much for granted. Frankie's father—as though hyper-aware of everything in his immediate surroundings or preternaturally capable of anticipating its approach—dipped, wove, feinted like Ali, spun around on the ball of one foot, and pointed with those blindingly white gloves the direction each motorist must go. He dazzled.

There were many others at that table besides Frankie: Tony, soft-spoken and gentle with an Afro like a thundercloud; bitter Daryle, who seemed eaten alive from the inside by his hatred of white people; sweet Homer; Kevin and Ernie; and fat Luther with his gold front teeth, who drove along the strip in his father's white on white in white Eldorado, with wide whitewalls, fuzzy dice, and scented with Strawberry Pimp Oil purchased exclusively at Axelrod Auto Parts. There was also Gary Lynn "Papa Doc" Dozier; William Williams, aka "Bill Bill"; Buffalo and Wolf; weird Ralph, who talked only to himself; and poor, retarded Clancy, who never talked at all but could smile in perfect, cross-eyed astonishment at whatever he heard.

And then there was practical-minded Dick Babb, who saved me once from a sure beating.

This was no small matter.

One night after football practice, I turned on someone who had been harassing me all day, calling me whitey and hunky and pushing me around. This was odd because the someone, Dwayne, wasn't a hostile fellow at all; he was a very mild and gentle guy. He wasn't a fighter in any sense of the word, which may explain why he chose me as an adversary. His locker was next to mine in the dressing room and he continued to give me a hard time after practice, until I spun around and glared at him. Then he pulled a *pencil*—yes!—and gestured as though to stab me.

We wrestled for that yellow no. 2, but he didn't put up much resistance. I shoved him back into his locker. We continued to wrestle around. His metal-tipped football cleats slipped on the concrete and he fell down, pulling me on top of him. I punched him a little halfheartedly. It was awkward and bumbling as neither of us were brawlers, and it was over almost as quickly as it began. The coach pulled us apart and sent us to the showers. Sore at each other still, we glared naked from opposite ends of the shower room, and then went home.

But the next morning everywhere I turned I found trouble. Every black kid in school, male and female alike, was talking shit about my "messing with" Dwayne. That the largest and toughest guys, who seemed like malevolent giants to me, eyed me with smoldering contempt was bad enough, but by midmorning, threats began: I was going to get my ass kicked, my ass was grass, I better watch my ass, etc., etc. And when confronted, the best I could muster were sputtered denials, which seemed only to make matters much worse.

Dick Babb and I often found ourselves sitting together in class or study hall, the last A and the first B. In study hall that day, Dick told me what to do, and it was perhaps the best boxing lesson anyone has ever given me in all of my life.

"Did you fight him?" he asked.

I nodded, a little apprehensive by then about that question.

"Did he start it?"

"Uh-huh."

"Did you kick his ass?"

"Well, yeah," I said, though this description seemed a little exaggerated. "More or less."

"What the fuck? 'More or less?'"

"OK, OK. I kicked his ass. And he deserved it because he'd messed with me all day."

"So, when somebody asks about it, just tell the truth," he said.

"You mean everyone already knows?" I said.

What an idea! It hadn't occurred to me that everyone among my antagonists knew exactly what happened in the locker room the previous evening.

"I think so," Dick said. "I know, and I wasn't there."

"So, everybody is just curious to see if I'll own up to it?"

"Something like that," Dick said and chuckled.

It wasn't long before the opportunity arrived to test this approach. Walking down the hall between classes someone grabbed me and threw me against the locker, pinning my shoulders to the door. It was an older student, Harold, right up in my face. A crowd gathered.

"Did you mess with my cuz?" he asked, staring me straight in the eye, his face close enough to kiss or bite me on the tip of the nose.

This was no time to miss a cue. I nodded.

"Dwayne messed with me all day, and then he pulled a pencil and tried to stab me."

"Did you kick his ass?"

"I kicked his ass."

That seemed to be all that he and the crowd wanted to hear.

He nodded and said, "OK."

The crowd assented to this version of events. A few even made disparaging remarks now about poor Dwayne! Roxanne, who was as big as a VW, cursed, "That goddamned Dwayne."

Harold let me go. "That's all I needed to know," he said and stepped back, releasing me. "Take it easy, man," he said and walked away. The crowd dispersed.

To say that I was amazed at the power of the truth to ease my troubled mind would be an understatement.

❦

The night Ali lost in the ring to Smokin' Joe Frazier, I sat in my room listening in amazement to my father's old Zenith Wavemagnet Trans-Oceanic shortwave radio, tubes glowing inside of its leather-covered box.

Ali was in good form through the first three rounds, but Frazier caught him out at the end of the third, snapping his head back with a hook, and then started in on Ali's body. From that point, my expectations proved flawed. Smokin' Joe put it to Ali, round after round, knocked his beautiful head off his shoulders, and then even knocked Ali down.

Knocked Ali down?

This was inconceivable. No one had ever so much as landed a blow before this night, or so I had convinced myself. Wasn't he invulnerable, invincible, godlike, returned from Olympus, choruses singing him Pindaric odes?

And yet, by the late rounds the announcers shouted through the speaker that Ali was *slumped* on the canvas. He was on his *knees*. He was *struggling* back onto his feet. They said he looked *dazed, subdued,* even *crushed* by the blows Frazier landed.

Then he *retreated,* trying just to *survive* to the bell. In the early rounds I tried to convince myself that Ali was putting us on, but it was evident his distress was no act. Both fighters' faces in the newspapers the next morning looked like tenderized meat.

❦

A month after the fight, as a manly field trip with pedagogical intention, my grandfathers performed a rare bipartisan service: pooling their mutual interests in my moral education, they took me to a closed-circuit rebroadcast of the fight in Canton.

My grandfather Axelrod had probably bet on Ali, and having lost a good sum of money, wanted to see for himself how his own assumptions had gone awry. My grandfather Peters, however, still gloated over Ali's demise, as it confirmed his long-held bias against my hero. He intended to use this opportunity to deepen my instruction in the finer points of self-defense. All the way along the highway to Canton, my grandfather Peters drummed the dash with delight, listening to WMMI and scatting along to Benny Goodman's solo in "Stompin' at the Savoy."

Square, butch-cut, fifty-year-old white men, a virtual VFW post, packed the seats at the Highway Cinema. I seemed to be the only person my age in attendance. The theater owner warmed us up with a reel of soft porn, and my grandfathers on either side of me tried to shield my eyes whenever a naked woman's ten-foot-tall breasts wobbled across the screen.

When it finally began, the brawl seemed as though it were acted out in a smoky, nightmarish cavern, where two grim men, unable to achieve the ecstasy of dance, stalked one another, crouched, elbows guarding their ribs, their muscled arms huge, glistening as they hooked and jabbed in brutal spasms. The two fighters, like the men watching them fight, battled to exhaustion, disfiguring not only themselves, but those for whose competing ideologies they fought and were convinced they must hate. In every seat in that theater, white men winced, ducked, sucked wind, and bobbed, taking punches through the screen. And when Ali fell, even with the plot already revealed, Frazier might just as well have killed and disemboweled him, then handed around his warm liver. I felt humiliated by my love for the joy I remembered once inhabited every word of Muhammad Ali's. I had placed him so high above us, when he fell it was as though he had thrown himself into the river that summer night in Louisville a decade earlier, vanquished forever.

Everything in my life up to that point had testified to the contrary, but I had imagined my hero, Muhammad Ali, exempt from miscalculation, from failure, from self-betrayal, and most improbably, exempt from time. Though my father's death had prepared me for how we could base our lives on folly, I'd set all that aside in the case of Muhammad Ali. Our pride may be scaled to romantic proportions, but pride disappoints because it leaves us vulnerable to the hostility, or worse, to the indifference that accompanies our demise, and not the hysterical choruses of bare-chested virgins we may prefer. Watching that fight only confirmed what listening to it had already established: a deep hole had opened in the world again, a hole it was reckless to ignore. Not only did my father get sucked into it, then my mother, but now even God, Muhammad Ali.

But those seated around us longed for something a bit more pedestrian. One man in the back of the theater having come unglued, crowed, "Kill the fucking nigger bastard! Kill him!"

~

Ali fought other fights as long and as brutal—the Thrilla in Manila, the Rumble in the Jungle—regained his title, lost it again, disgraced by his former sparring partner Leon Spinks. And still he didn't quit but stumbled after an inflated Vegas purse against a third-rate no-account, Trevor Berbick, a fighter so dull he couldn't off Ali, finish him right there in the ring, but instead embarrassed the punch-drunk fool, who shuffled along, a sad, old, thick-tongued boxer, his words slurred, his mind seemingly lost in haze. Was this the man who once brought back gold from the Olympics, and spent it all too early crossing a river too wide, too poisoned by hatred for any of us to cross to the other side? This all occurred well before Ali's rehabilitation in the American mind, long before he lit the Olympic torch in Atlanta, long before he began to appear in Louis Vuitton ads in the *New Yorker*, long before he was portrayed by sycophantic actors in Hollywood biopics or became the subject of fawning reminiscences of well-pedigreed liberals. This all occurred when he was still the object of America's hatred and contempt, that is, if anyone noticed him at all. There was a time not all that long ago when someone might have asked, "I wonder whatever became of Muhammad Ali?"

I had no words then for what becomes of even beautiful men betrayed by stubborn reality. But leaving that theater with my grandfathers on a balmy night in May, I vowed to allow no one and nothing I loved to pass from this life without praise, even if I must praise the most bewildering losses.

THE EVIDENCE OF THINGS NOT SEEN

On a recent April morning, my cousin Betty Mills and I walked back to the Wright place together in the rain. The Wrights were an African American farm family, my grandmother's and her siblings' neighbors when they were still children in the 1920s. The Wrights preceded our family on that ridge in the Appalachian foothills of Ohio by at least a generation. My grandmother's brother, William, was only the second Mills to farm there; the grandfather purchased the Chambers' farm in the aftermath of the Civil War. Since my childhood, when I first heard anecdotes about the Wrights, they have loomed large in my reveries. Over the years, whenever I "go down home," to use my grandmother's preferred expression for visiting the farm, I've taken time to walk to the site, forested now, where the Wrights' cabin and barn once stood.

After dinner the evening before our walk, Betty and I were standing on the top landing of the central staircase facing a low chest of drawers, from which Betty pulled out a folder bound in string. Inside was a letter she handed to me, saying, "I think this might interest you." Owing to the revelations of that letter recently discovered in the attic of the old farmhouse, and despite our walking along the familiar farm lane we'd walked together many times before, I was seeing the world around me with new eyes.

The uncancelled two-cent stamp on the envelope dated the composition of the letter inside to sometime between 1919 and 1928, though there's good reason to believe it dates from earlier in that period of time. The Millses—Betty's grandparents—were the recipients. The heavy, printed capital letters seem to have been composed with a carpenter's pencil, and each flat stroke making up a grapheme was written over a second time before moving on to the next stroke. The circular, embossed two-cent stamp, with white lettering over red ink and George Washington's silhouette at its center, had the letters *KKK* written along the upper right-hand edge of the stamp. The letter is addressed: "TO THE INSANE FARM AND COLORED INFIRMIARY [*sic*]." I unfolded the stationery inside; its edges were periodically missing wedges, cut out with scissors—two wedges from the top and bottom and three from both the left and right edges—to create a sense, I imagined, of menace, albeit a cartoonish sort of menace for sure. At the top margin was a drawn image of a manicule pointing ominously toward a skull and crossbones and the word "BEWARE." "BEWARE." The remaining text, all in capital letters, with many letters reversed, confirms the implacable dread the top line intended to provoke: "ON OR BEFORE SUNRISE OF APRIL 17—YOU WILL BOTH BE BURNED TO DEATH OR *SHOT* TO PAY THE PENALTY FOR BURNING THREE BARNS AND TRYING TO KILL THE COX FAMILY." It was signed, "K.K.K." The addressees seem, at least in part, inconsistent with the accusation and threat being lodged. If the Millses were in any way suspected of burning down the Coxes' barns or otherwise presenting an existential threat to that family, why then drag the African American neighbors—presumably the Wrights or others living nearby—into this quarrel?

Betty had told me a year before our walk that April morning that the barn at the top of the farm lane today was the Wrights' barn, moved from its original foundations to its present site only after her father, William, purchased the Wrights' former property during the Second World War. I didn't know then that the original barn had burned down, much less the reason why. Nor did she.

We might wonder how Harvey and Elizabeth Mills responded to the threat. Elizabeth, as proper a Presbyterian lady as ever there was, made her feelings famously clear when she referred to the source of the threat as "those Cox suckers." Given the two references to the KKK and inventive racial epithet with the added syllable, one wonders if the accusation is simply a pretext for something else entirely, that is, racist contempt for whatever relations—practical, if not cordial—may or may not have existed between the Mills and the Wright families during the era of Jim Crow.

There's another unpleasant anecdote regarding Elizabeth that may be related to these matters and perhaps sheds light on racial tensions in rural Ohio in the early twentieth century. The now elderly daughter-in-law of my grandmother's sister, Myrtle, recently wrote to Betty: "As for the Wright family, you probably heard the same story that there was a knock on the back door and Elizabeth called out, 'If you are white come in, if you are black, stay out.' Only to find Mr. Wright at the door." It's a strange incident to remember, perhaps even stranger to expect others to recognize it not as explicitly racist and humiliating for all parties involved, but as some kind of benign, somehow comic or even quirky, family anecdote.

It's also weird how these two scraps of anecdotes regarding Elizabeth Mills—vulgar and mean-spirited—are all that remain of this supposedly most proper Presbyterian lady's own spoken words. Are they memorable, we might ask, because they are otherwise so out of character? That seems to be the family consensus. In any event, neither Harvey nor Elizabeth were murdered by or before sunrise on April 17, 1920-something-or-other. Harvey died of respiratory disease in 1926, and Elizabeth of cancer in 1935. In retribution for their offenses, however, their barn was burned to the ground by the letter-writers.

❧

Spring arrived late this year in Ohio and the trees were still not leafed out as Betty and I walked across the fields toward the forest south of the barn. The lane we were walking along turned to follow the edge of the woods, where a few small dogwoods glowed white against the gray.

Like so much else in rural America, that farm is a story of displacements. What forests remain are third- or fourth-growth trees, whose virgin stands began falling a lifetime before our family's arrival on that ridge. It's clear how profit has been wrung from the land in every way possible. Nothing alive has been left alone, left to its own purposes. The forests have been repeatedly logged and cleared and the fields surface-mined for low-quality, sulfurous coal then leveled, tiled, and more recently, hydraulically fracked for oil and natural gas extracted from the Utica shale deeper below the surface. The land ethic, if you dare even to call it such, is one of economic desperation, of doing whatever is necessary for the family to survive in the moment and remain on the land for a while longer, until another profitable abuse against what is alive can be discovered. As with the flora, and the mineral and water resources, any notion of wildness among the megafauna there has been diminished by generations of its absence. The white-tailed deer are plentiful enough, uniquely adapted as they are to fragmented habitats, but the elk, black bear, timber wolves, and large cats that once roamed there have fled.

Walking along the edge of forest and plowed ground with Betty, it was easy to see the consequences of so much soil and subsoil being pushed around. Sealed tight and airless at the surface, the soil in the fields is yellow clay mixed with a layer of stony detritus, a far cry from the rich, dark loamy soils that once lay many feet deep before being cleared and put to the plow.

In a grove of honey locust trees just off the lane we stood before the ruins of the Wright place. My uncle William, my grandmother's younger brother and Betty's father, purchased the Wright place from Paul Oyer in 1942, who purchased it from the executor of the Wright's estate in the late 1930s. My uncle's "purchase" I think was more likely an exchange—he got the land after helping his friend, Paul Oyer, clear-cut the timber.

The Wrights who lived there during the childhood of my grandmother and her siblings were the children of Winifred (Cyrus) and William, born slaves in Virginia early in the 1820s. They seemed to possess a much deeper and historically richer claim to that land than the Millses. They owned and farmed it, after all, *before* the Civil War, during which William Wright died in defense of the Union, fighting for the freedom of others as a member of the 17th regiment of US Colored Troops. Having known its absence, freedom for the Wrights, as we might imagine it, was no noble-minded abstraction, but a profoundly lived reality. Their presence on that ridge *prior* to the Civil War also resonates with a more complex reality. No one, least of all my racist male cousins (I'll get to them soon enough), have given that fact or its ethical significance much thought.

After the war, Winifred was the sole landholder of this property—a woman and former slave, farming and raising her children alone. She strikes me as a truly remarkable person about whom we know almost nothing else. Two of her children, Millie and Phoebe, and on occasion, their brother William L., were an important and benevolent presence in the lives of my grandmother and especially of her younger siblings, Ann and Helen. The Wrights' prominent place in our family's history seems uncharacteristic, as my grandmother's family has no other relations with African

Americans, who are now few and far between in rural Ohio. And little wonder—driving to the farm, I passed innumerable Make America Great Again signs alongside confederate flags, which is cosmically ironic given the history of the area as a former abolitionist stronghold, dotted with clandestine stops along the underground railroad.

Though my better-educated, more worldly relatives may be sensitive to those ironies and tolerant if not progressively minded about issues related to race, the political views of many other family members are, to put it charitably, somewhat less than generous. My mother's response to this dynamic is telling. After my father's early departure from life, she soon found herself at the center of the local civil rights movement, and often in the company of new black friends and lovers. By the late 1960s we were hiding Black Panthers in the basement of our suburban home on Pleasant Place. During the intervening years, she has stopped attending the annual family reunions because the gleeful racist grotesqueries of the men go unchallenged in the era of Trump, who has emboldened them in their moral sloth.

For me, the Wrights and their "place" are a much more complicated and truer American story than the one white families, my own included, typically tell about themselves.

All my life, I've returned in reverie to those ruins, hoping to catch a glimpse of the Wrights. My grandmother and her siblings, when they were still quite young, lived and worked in the daily presence of the Wrights and often tried to describe that shared experience. The fragments of memory they struggled to piece together into stories never quite took shape and have since grown only more inaccessible. Losing touch with the living memory of the Wrights, we lose touch with ourselves.

My great-great-grandfather purchased that farm next to the Wrights for his ne'er-do-well son, Harvey, and only Harvey and his son, William, who took over at the age of thirteen when Harvey died, farmed there for their entire lives. By the time Betty's younger brother left the farm and farming altogether, she had taken early retirement and returned to live in and restore the old farmhouse where she and her brothers, Austin and Edward, grew up. Because there are no heirs willing to or capable of farming those three hundred-odd impoverished acres—the limitations on desire such work demands being a huge disincentive—and because now that my grandmother's generation—Betty's parent's generation—have either passed away or slipped into dementia, those of us who remain bear sole responsibility for the memory that will outlast us there. Soon we will have been displaced, joining the accretions of absence that reach back far beyond the Civil War or the frontier, beyond even the time the Delaware Indians lay claim to east-central and northeast Ohio, and deeper still, at least a thousand years before the present, when the Hopewell culture flourished in the great forests that once grew across those hills. We're poised to permanently depart from this place; the evidence of our lives, of things no longer seen, will pass forever into the night of time.

～

Who were the Wrights? Besides a few anecdotes, it's been hard for us to agree. Betty's genealogical search established the dates of birth and death for both William Wright (1824–1865) and his wife, Winifred Cyrus (1823–1913), and that they and their children lived on the farm adjacent to ours. Early the next morning at Betty's kitchen table, following a series of clicks through websites, I found myself looking at a recent photograph of Winifred Wright's well-kept gravestone in the nearby Hope Cemetery in Salem, Ohio. Her grave, it turned out, is tended by Gayle Ormes Hawthorne. This came as a surprise. Though his connection to the Wrights and the reason he appeared in the Mills family memory had never been clear to us, Emmet Ormes was long a vivid presence in the fragments of memory about the Wrights. I contacted Gayle, she soon wrote back, and our correspondence filled in the gaps in both families' understanding of the past and proved nothing short of astonishing.

No one could be more remarkable than Winifred Wright's parents, the long-lived Edinborough Cyrus (1764–1854) and even longer-lived Amelia Gray Cyrus (1780–1889), whose daughter married William Wright on September 16, 1846. Both Winifred's parents were born slaves, her father in Culpepper, Virginia, her mother in Maryland. According to Gayle, her great-great grandfather was a barber who purchased his freedom and the freedom of his wife and their eight children in 1824, when he was sixty, Amelia forty-four, and Winifred one year old. Two more children, John and Lavina, were born free in Ohio. Given their ages and determination to bring their family out of slavery and form a family in freedom, there can be little doubt Gayle was correct when she observed, with considerable understatement, that her forbears, Edinborough and Amelia, were "hard working . . . and family was important."

After all, Ohio may have entered the Union as a free state in 1803, but it did everything possible to restrict the migration of African Americans from the south. Very likely slaves were owned in more remote areas of southern Ohio, and though southern slave owners who moved to Ohio may have freed their slaves when they came north, those former slaves often continued to work in their former owners' households. According to R. Douglas Hurt's *The Ohio Frontier, 1720–1830,* "southern immigrants brought African Americans, particularly women, into Ohio as indentured servants. Black children were often indentured until the age of twenty-one." Through the late eighteenth and early nineteenth centuries, fugitive slaves sometimes found refuge among local tribes. Slave owners seem to have been reluctant to demand the return of their "property" from tribes, who no doubt would have responded to such proprietary claims with a hostile irony that even perhaps slave owners understood.

The Black Codes expressed the racial prejudice that prevailed in the "free" territory and later the "free" state of Ohio. These laws required African Americans, like Edinbourgh and Amelia Cyrus and their children, to prove they were free and not runaway slaves. The laws also required African Americans to have two sponsors who could put up five hundred dollars as a guarantee of acceptable character and future behavior. The franchise was denied black men by one vote, cast by Edward Tiffin, southern immigrant, former slave-owner, and soon-to-be first governor of Ohio. Miscegenation laws were passed, and African Americans were forbidden to own firearms. It wasn't until 1849 that a coalition of the Democratic and Free Soil parties helped to repeal these laws. Perhaps this explains the growth of the African American population, which between 1800 and 1820 grew from a few hundred to almost five thousand. By 1860, there were perhaps as many as thirty-seven thousand African Americans in Ohio. In addition, as many as one hundred thousand fugitive slaves moved through Ohio to Canada along the Underground Railroad, which was very active in the vicinity of our family farm. Many nearby towns provided safe haven. That fugitives crossed our land and the land belonging to the Wrights seems likely, as nearby Hanoverton was an important stop along the Underground Railroad, where brick tunnels connected houses of prominent citizens, and the Sandy and Beaver Canal boats offered escape toward the next stop in Salem. That so few of these runaways chose to remain in the "free state" of Ohio is evidence of the prevailing dangers of American institutional racism.

William and Winifred had a large family of their own—Lucretia, Laura, Linneous, Luella, Jesse, Amelia, William L., and Phoebe. Laura would marry Othean Ormes. Only Amelia (aka "Millie"), Phoebe, and William L. appear in the Millses' memory, although Emmet is among the three children of Othean and Laura Ormes. Gayle provided an additional insight about Emmet's presence on the farm. His mother Laura, after the death of Othean, took care of her mother, and after Laura's death, Emmet moved in with his elderly grandmother. Winifred died in 1913, when Betty's father, William Mills, was still an infant. Emmet, Gayle pointed out, soon married and moved away, but later returned to the area.

❧

Why have the Wrights and Ormeses remained so dear in memory that, despite the racism of some of my male relatives, the women have felt compelled over the last century to remember their connection to my great aunts, Ann and Helen, when they were still girls? Everything we know that's been gathered from documentary sources about the Wrights, Cyruses, and Ormeses is piecemeal at best. Phoebe, for example, was educated. We know this from an article in the *Standard Free Press* extolling the perfect annual attendance of my grandmother and her siblings at the Green Grove school, which then lists the "history of this school," consisting of a list of graduates. At the bottom of that list we read: "Phoebe Wright, a colored girl, a pupil of this school, received a certificate as a teacher, [but] never taught." She was certainly no girl at the time my grandmother attended that same school. We might wonder, though, where in the world she would have been permitted to teach during the era of Jim Crow, when the local idealism of the previous century had soured into the unreconstructed racism that persists there to this day. The few other glimpses of Phoebe that we have suggest that she, and to a degree, her sister Millie, played an important adult, if not parental, role in the early lives of my great aunts.

Before she died, Ann recalled for her daughter, Sally, that "Phoebe was very outgoing." Others have made the point of recalling that she was "slender." Phoebe "liked the out of doors," and "did the outside work." Whereas Millie, who was a "homebody and seldom left the house" in Ann's stories, was predictably "heavy set." It was Millie, naturally, who gave Ann a recipe from which Ann made her first cake and all subsequent cakes—cake I have eaten. We learn from Sally's records that Ann "would go out in the woods with Phoebe . . . [who] would show you different kinds of berries, etc., tell you what they were and if you could eat them. Mom would help her pick cherries and gather eggs." Little doubt then that it was Phoebe who first took the Mills children to the "Big Rock" on the Wright Place, farther down the stream that ran past their house. Ann described the rock as having "a big enough overhang to keep out of the rain."

Ann addressed the issue of race, but only to say that when she "was young she didn't even notice [the Wrights] were black." She would hold up her arm next to theirs and say, "I have more suntan than you do." This may reveal, more than Ann's childish naiveté, that the Wrights were of mixed race, though no one ever mentioned this until Gayle wrote that "many in the family were light-skinned, so they were at times accepted in the communities where they lived. However, people knew they were people of color." These moments from a summer long ago reveal that the Wright sisters played both casual and engaged daily roles in the upbringing of my grandmother's generation, which in large part must account for the women's enduring affection for and allegiance to their memory of the Wrights, elided as those memories may be.

～

Betty and I stood in the lane, the Wright Place just off in the woods to our left. If you didn't know to look there, you might not see it, partly buried under decades of leaves, fallen trees, wild grape vine, mayapple, skunk cabbage, floribunda, blackberry brambles, and thick layers of moss that have draped the foundation stones in glistening green. The place appeared as lovely to me as ever. Though I returned often in reverie, I visited the Wright place perhaps on one occasion only during childhood. I recall bouncing along the lane one summer day, sitting on a wagon pulled behind a tractor William drove. When we stopped, those who knew the Wrights spoke about them to my cousin Austin and me. Who else was there? My grandparents, William, and possibly his wife, Margaret, all spoke. Perhaps Betty and her younger brother Edward also listened. The moment was otherwise indelible, given the unusual formality of getting us all there for the specific purpose of sharing the names of those who were absent. In my early twenties, I wrote a poem in the imperative voice that opens by describing the approach along the farm lane that day long ago:

> Follow the grassy lane a quarter mile
> below the barn, down along the cattail shore
> of the Army Corps of Engineers bass pond,
> follow overgrown fencerows
> across pastures deep in orchard grass,
> and step into a stand of honey locust
> that canopy between us and sky,
> casting shadows skittish as fry below,
> sunlight twirling on touch-me-not.

I had the impression years later, when Betty and I skied to the Wright place one December evening, that some sort of mining was going on farther down the lane—a violation in my mind of what had become a sacred place. When I last visited the farm thirty-one years ago, I also walked back to the Wright place, but all I remember from that day was looking at the new field, a steep hillside just to the west of the lane that William had cleared for pasture with his prized Army Surplus bulldozer. When William died, Austin planted trees that are large enough now to form a canopy over the open, grassy forest floor below, glowing green on that rainy morning in April. Betty was pleased with her little brother's decision to put the hillside back into woods, as it had been her responsibility to hay it during her summer vacations from teaching—a dangerous and unpleasant task, given the precarious slope. Her adult brother's life has not unfolded altogether happily, but seeing that hillside in grass and trees, seeing this gesture of healing he intended there—and surely that is what it was—it's the living embodiment of what he saw in his mind, but didn't remain there long enough to see restored, as surely I and everyone else would wish for him to be healed and restored the same in that place.

⤜

On Monday, October 18, 1942, "promptly at 12:00 noon," William held a public sale. The poster advertising that sale is framed and hanging on the wall beside the front entry to the house. "As I have been drafted into the army I will sell at public auction on my farm," the poster reads, then lists his assets. In anticipation of his absence, whether temporary or permanent, he liquidated his stock and machinery. Among those items sold were "Gray Team 9 and 11 years old, sound and good workers, a good logging team." Also, included in the sale were nine head of cattle, fifty head of hogs, thirty-nine head of sheep, "about" one hundred chickens, and a machinery barn full of implements, plus "about 25 tons of good hay; 450 bu. oats; 250 bu. wheat; 50 bu. buckwheat; around 100 baskets of old corn; 15 acres of good standing corn, 28 acres of wheat in the ground; about 50 bu. potatoes." Good lord, one can only wonder at the effect this loss had on the man's sense of himself and his regard for the colossally violent world into which he was being sent. He was a thirteen-year-old, after all, when he was pulled out of school and forced to take over the farm, a formative experience that Betty thinks "stuck with him his whole life." I don't think she meant that in a good way, either. He would refer to himself "as just a dumb farmer," which is the sort of thing people say about themselves when they know it's not true but the result of circumstances others who might judge them are ignorant of. Saying so was a way to dare people finer than himself to agree.

Among the last things he did before shipping out was to walk to the Wright place, where, on the door of the Wrights' former cabin, he posted this curt note for the curious to consider: "You son of a bitch, stay the hell out of here."

There are other brief glimpses of the Wrights and Emmet Ormes. William Mills, for example, "took Phoebe to Carrollton to pay her taxes," possibly in a cart drawn by that "good team," later sold at auction. William also helped the Wrights butcher in exchange for them doing the same for him. We know from Ann and my grandmother that both families joined to help with each other's threshing in the fall. Gayle Ormes fills in another gap here. Edinborough's sons, Thomas, William L., Edinborough Jr., and John ran a nearby gristmill, to which we might conclude the young William Mills still may have hauled his grain to be ground.

Two other stories of William Mills's relate to Emmet, whose role in William's early life seems as vivid as Phoebe's and Winnie's during the youth of my aunt Ann, although a good deal more conflicted. Emmet apparently took great pleasure in chronically cleaning William's clock at checkers, the older man allowing the boy to continue exposing himself to an eventual run of the board, accompanied by the older man's laughter. "I'm sorry son, but I'm afraid you've lost this one, too." Another story is about a moment when Emmet exposed himself as well. I assume it took place during Prohibition, when Emmet seems to have indulged a little too much of the local moonshine and was discovered running naked across the fields and lawn outside our farmhouse under the summer stars. William Mills, being the man of the house, was summoned to lead his neighbor, the happy dancer, home and put him to bed. Unlike Elizabeth's surviving words, there is about these two stories, as with those recounted by my great aunts, an undercurrent of respect for the ethics of ordinary neighborliness that transcends age and race. To this day, the latter story elicits something like a rhetorical blush in our family, though I don't believe for a second that my great-uncle William ever blushed. Predictably, my cousin recently communicated to me that William, his mother's son for sure, referred to his erstwhile companion with the usual racial epithets, the same as his younger male relations throw about casually today. Still, the two men lived full lives in the world that was available to them, and I can only hope that each felt grudging respect, if not affection, for the other that I wish to feel for them.

~&~

The cabin on which William posted his warning to trespassers has long since been moved to Hanoverton. Only the cellar hole remains, the outline of what I presume was the kitchen and the springhouse just above. From the spring, a small stream flows just south of where the house stood. The Wrights would have heard it at night as they fell asleep and again in the morning when they woke. The barn, visible a quarter mile away on the ridge to which it was moved long after the arson attack, stood not fifty feet from the Wrights' house, on the northwest corner of the property, next to the lane, and against a high bank that would have allowed easy access to the hayloft. The foundations are a jumble of quarried stones. In among the forest detritus Betty and I found the leather remains of a harness and the toe of an old pair of brogues. We also uncovered what must be the metal pieces of hames and a broken crock, all of which we hid again under the leaves so that curious "sons of bitches" don't carry it away.

On the slope below the foundation of the house there are large patches of daffodils and day lilies that must have grown in the flower gardens the Wrights or their forebears planted over two centuries ago.

⌑

As I drove along the road to the farm, I wondered what kind of world the Mills and Wright families shared? When the car emerged from the forested hollow, the fields on the ridge opened as always, a foot deep in lush green annual rye. At the blind turn, I paused and waited, as I was taught long ago, to make certain no oncoming vehicle was hidden in the dip below the crest of the hill. I turned left onto the white gravel of the township road and turned next up the farm lane under the old pines and horse chestnuts that seemed no different to me than fifty years ago. Alongside the lane, Betty has added flower beds, full now of spring beauties and phlox. Halfway up the lane, between the township road and the barn on the low ridge above, stands the house, built in Federal style by the Chambers family, previous owners of the farm.

The Chambers family may have been fashioned from finer timber than the Millses. The Chamberses were the sort of nineteenth-century farm family, after all, who published their matriarch's literary works: *Poems of Elizabeth Shreve Chambers: Sketches of Her Life and Reminiscences*, on page ninety-one of which appear these verses, from a much longer poem, "To the Memory of James H. Chambers (1816–1891)" who built the house and owned the farm we refer to as "down home": "The house was built in modern style, / Of brick the walls were made, / And the long, large stones in the cellar wall / Were neat and substantially laid." It's a treat to find one's own home memorialized in a rough metrical approximation of same meter as one finds in the Protestant hymnal. The actual provenance of the poem, though, is a little murky, as it's credited not to Elizabeth, in whose collected writings it appears, but to the son of the James H. Chambers of the title—presumably Elizabeth's son.

The house is much as depicted in the poem. A two-storied, red brick rectangle, it reflects the rationalized, tripartite design of Enlightenment-era architecture—aka "modern style" circa 1850 in rural east-central Ohio. The house is two very high-ceilinged rooms deep, and two rooms broad, with a central hall and staircase between wings. At the back of the house, there is an enclosed porch. Also in the back of the house, there are additional small rooms on either end of the porch, pantries off the kitchen and summer kitchen, one of which was Betty's playroom when she was a girl, and is restored now as a second pantry. The front door opens onto a porch and a large quarried sandstone pad two steps high, overlooking the lawn sloping down toward the township road.

Elizabeth Chambers' sister-in-law, Mrs. Mary J. (Chambers) Neill, is the subject of a short biography that appeared in the local *Free Press Standard*, dated March 18, 1899. The article throws some light on what life in and around our family farm would have been like in the early nineteenth century through the time of the Civil War and after. She recalls that her father "had all of his teeth sound and perfect when he died." She recalls that in the country surrounding the farm during her childhood, "Deer and wolves were numerous." She also "remembers of having seen Indian wigwams and camps."

The article is accompanied by a photograph of a smiling, slender, and alert-eyed elderly woman in a dark, high-collared, long-sleeved black dress. She has extraordinarily long fingers. And she is extraordinary for having had "her education . . . looked after more carefully than most of the girls of her day." That's to say, she attended the local one-room school house as well as "a few terms" of college in the town of Mount Pleasant. This would likely have been Franklin College, which the official Harrison County website recalls "was a hotbed of abolitionist sentiment and teaching during the years leading up to the Civil War." The college's founder, Reverend John Walker, was a Presbyterian minister and "staunch abolitionist . . . [who] taught the abolitionist doctrine and many of the graduates carried the message forward in their careers as ministers, teachers, or attorneys." The Chambers seem to have been Quakers, however, and so the common thread in her education was abolitionist ethics rather than denominational allegiance.

The college she attended for those two terms had many notable graduates, among them Reverend Titus Basfield, who, like the Wrights, had been born a slave and was among the first African Americans to graduate from an Ohio college. The Harrison County website recalls another prominent graduate, John A. Bingham, who as a congressional representative ushered legislation through the Congress that eventually became the Fourteenth Amendment to the United States Constitution. It was Bingham who "ensured the inclusion of the Equal Protection Clause with Reverend Basfield and his family in mind." Though the amendment was adopted by Ohio and the other states in the immediate aftermath of the war, it was revoked by the Ohio legislature in 1868 and not reauthorized until 2003. This disgraceful episode in Ohio history is being repeated today as candidates who recently ran for the Republican presidential nomination called for the repeal of the Fourteenth Amendment. The Trump Administration's subsequent travel ban has specifically tried to undermine the legal authority of this amendment. That travel ban was recently upheld by a 5–4 vote in the US Supreme Court—a sad commentary on our era's malice.

Edinborough Cyrus, who was born a slave and led his family to freedom, is buried in the Augusta cemetery, only a few miles from our farm. Next to him lies his son-in-law, William Wright, who died fighting for the Union and the freedom for which that

Union is the guarantor. In our subsequent correspondence, Gayle wrote, "I feel that the three families"—the Cyruses, Ormeses, and Wrights—"were well-respected in their communities." We can only wish that such respect existed in those same communities today. "A few years back," she wrote, "the Augusta Cemetery honored William Wright for his service in the Civil War." I have driven past that cemetery all my life. Betty and I drove past it in April—twice. It's just north of Route 9, on a hillside behind the Presbyterian Church. We passed each time unaware that these two men who are so fundamental to our understanding of ourselves and our sense of the place lay close by.

Gayle wrote again to say that she had been in Augusta recently to visit the two graves. How did she feel, I wonder, driving through territory so openly hostile toward her? Her claim to the place is as deep, if not much deeper, than anyone alive today. Those two men, fundamental to her own history, made their dream of the possibility of her life and the lives of her children and grandchildren a reality. Those men also are our clear link to leaps in America's ethical history, leaps of national moral conscience that are nearly the sole provenance of African Americans, who demanded that the nation that carried them away into captivity live up to the professed ideals of its foundational documents. Is that really asking too much? Though the future was unseen by them, Edinborough Cyrus and William Wright placed their faith in it and the ideals, if not the practice, of the nation they and millions of black men and women like them built and defended. As she drove to Augusta from Salem the previous summer, Gayle would have passed by our farm unaware that it's the very place where the Wrights lived and farmed and where her life founded itself in freedom.

A NOTE LEFT ON A MOUNTAIN

On June 23, 2003, the BBC reported: "'Birth cry' of the cosmos heard." Mark Whittle, a professor of astronomy at the University of Virginia, appears in a photograph at the head of the article with a spoon in his right hand and an empty wine glass in his left to illustrate, somewhat oddly, the discovery and recording of this "birth cry." Whittle, we learn, "analyzed the so-called background radiation that was born four hundred thousand years after the Big Bang." Whittle explains that the "ripples in the radiation" resemble sound waves thirty thousand light-years wide and fifty-five octaves below the threshold of human hearing. Whittle "shifted" these inaudible sound waves to the audible range of human hearing to create two sound recordings available on the Internet. The first renders the initial million years of the expanding universe as five seconds of what, it's hard to say precisely, though it's surely fascinating. Noise, yes, but despite being noise, it manages somehow to please. The second, somewhat longer, compresses the sound of the first four hundred thousand years, a sound, the article explains, that "changes from a bright major chord to a somber minor one."

That's no literary fancy. Listening to it reminded me of the first piece of classical music I was in any way consciously aware of—Beethoven's Seventh Symphony, the second movement in particular, the Allegretto, which I would listen to repeatedly as a young child. After reading about this cosmological birth cry, I listened to the symphony all the way through twice, then listened a third time to the Allegretto, whose "pale key of A minor," suggests a worldly reality far more difficult and troubling than the joyful Vivace of the first movement, once referred to as the "apotheosis of dance." As the Allegretto begins, its melancholy strings seem to recognize our fate, possibly all fates, as uniformly serious and grave. Thinking again of Whittle's discovery in his second rendering of genesis, it's as if God recognized too late a flaw in His universal design.

Listening to those universal soundscapes and to Beethoven's Seventh Symphony, I realized how despite the pleasure of their novelty, the brevity of Whittle's recordings disappoints. Who wouldn't wish for those cosmic recordings to continue? Who but those in despair wouldn't wish for this brief but novel life to linger a little longer? Besides the fact that neither of Whittle's recordings is particularly beautiful, those inconceivably distant chords provoke an odd comfort—an ambient tone, the background radiation, if you will, of the universal mother's pulse heard inside the cosmological womb.

❧

Ask someone, "Do you recall your birth?" and you will be regarded strangely. So, ask again: "No, really, do you remember?"

I once asked this question to someone who claimed she had no memories at all prior to turning eighteen and leaving home, a claim so preposterous, I ceased all contact with her at that instant. A childhood friend, Moritz, once claimed that he recalled a dream he associated with being ill, his first high fever. Before the fever broke, he was aware of himself trapped in a carmine-lit room whose walls were like a membrane collapsing around him.

He felt awkward as a giant in a world built for a Lilliputian, and the tiny scale of things felt suffocating, requiring him to stoop, fold himself in half as the ceilings lowered around his head and shoulders.

"A terrifying dream," he said. "And no apparent way out of that room." He told me that he heard a sound, deep-toned and distant, throbbing through the walls. A sound so familiar and pleasant that he felt even more conflicted about his panicked need to exit the shrinking room. He wished to remain in the presence of the sound, but to have lingered any longer would have caused him to pass out. Then the fever broke, and the dream ended; Moritz woke in his bed alone, covered in sweat, the only other sounds being the voices of his mother and sister going about their daily lives elsewhere in the house and a crow cawing from a bare maple outside his window.

The sound of the mother's heart, obviously, isn't the sound of the universe. Not exactly. And yet, the intensity with which Moritz recalled the intimacy of his mother's body and his own desire to live was unsettling, especially in light of subsequent discoveries.

His memory of a time before his own consciousness of time reminded me of another conversation we had, in which he explained Leopardi's argument concerning the resonant depths of collective memory, the "beauty and pleasure" of that memory accumulating inside of words. Such memories, Moritz explained, as are perhaps aroused whenever we use a common name for a plant or animal. Arthur Sze's list of endangered or extinct species in his poem "The String Diamond" is a poignant example of Leopardi's (and Moritz's) claim: "bluemask darter, / crested honeycreeper, / rough-leaved loosestrife." Even in the eternal absence of extinction, the memory of the living thing's "beauty and pleasure" lives on in the uttered name. In *The Dominion of the Dead*, Robert Pogue Harrison summarizes Leopardi's argument: "the worlds our words once inhabited re-inhabit in turn the words that outlive them." And so, we listen hopefully for the song of origins we recall being sung to us inside both the mother's, as well as the cosmological, womb.

In Moritz's case, however, it was more complicated. His miraculous memory of birth in no way lessened the burden of what we understood was his family's recent history and the cause of his melancholy. Though he was born in the United States, in 1958, the silence his German parents maintained about the past, specifically the wordless world of that catastrophically violent period prior to their emigration, inhabited and disturbed every aspect of his life and rendered futile any effort to rescue him from despair.

It took me an hour searching boxes in a storage unit to find something I had jotted down in a journal not long before Moritz disappeared from all but memory and words. Exactly twenty years before the publication of "'Birth cry' of the cosmos heard," that is, on June 23, 1983, my seven-week-old child asleep in the bed beside me on Bear Creek in Montana, I woke to a sound of distant, low-pitched humming. I lay there in wonder. That sound I could feel as well as hear lasted perhaps no more than a few seconds in the borderlands of sleep, though its presence filled ten thousand years or more. I put my sleeping child back in his cradle, went to the kitchen, and wrote the following at 5:15 a.m.:

> In the first light, the roar of God, then the singing of small birds. I could hear it coming down from across the fields. I caught a chill but decided to get up anyway and see what was outside. It seemed familiar, that sound toward which we're draw for comfort, as to the sound of our own heart resounding in the pillow as we fall asleep, an echo of the sound of our mother's heart all around us before we're born. One heart beating within another within another. I walked out along the lane, under a canopy of aspens, and gazed over the hayfields, at that moment full of daisies, and I distinctly remember

thinking that I could *see* the sound I heard, like an animation of radio signals transmitted not from a steel tower, but from the Sapphire Mountains, in whose foothills I stood.

At 10:30 a.m., after walking down the road to retrieve the morning newspaper, I added: "Opened the *Missoulian* to the peaceful faces of three decapitated Salvadorans."

That afternoon, Josefa and I, infant son in tow, searched for Moritz, who had abandoned his apartment and belongings in Missoula. We caught a glimpse of what we thought was his car on the county road below a bridge on I-90, exited the highway, and followed him to a room in a motel in East Missoula. He refused at first to answer the door. We pleaded. Finally, he threw the deadbolt, opened the door, and agreed to come with us.

Within an hour, Moritz had set up residence in a pup tent outside of our cabin.

Before we went to sleep that evening, I recorded this final entry for June 23, 1983: "Uncle Hans passed away tonight. The first loss of this sort since the death of my grandfather, seven years ago, and before that, my father, twenty-one years ago. It's sad to realize that given how old the aunts and uncles are this is the first in a long series of losses to follow."

Subsequently, I forgot the broad sweep of that day and its melancholy intimacies, but never the sound I heard that morning.

⁓

After a close call with my own death in my mid-thirties, I met Richard McFarland, who lived alone without phone or electricity far down the Imnaha River. I had earlier expressed to a friend my desire to meet people who abandoned the lives they created to return to the lost landscapes of childhoods. A friend of my friend supplied Richard's "address" in that remote canyon. It's a striking landscape, the one he was hoping to reclaim. Canyon walls of ochre-colored columnar basalt are interspersed with broad grassy benches that rise thousands of feet above the canyon floor, where a primitive road winds above the river. From that rough road, the broad western sky narrows to a channel of blue, mirroring the river below. Depending on the season, the road is either rutted, muddy, or dusty as it divides into various trails leading to backcountry ranches and camps.

Having never traveled into the area, I arranged through a series of letters over several months to meet Richard at the mouth of Lightning Creek. At the appointed time, he stood waiting, leaning against his flatbed truck and contemplatively smoking a pipe of tobacco. When he saw me in the twilight, he leaned forward and shoved his tall, thin frame away from the front fender of his truck. He gestured to follow along a dirt track that led through galleries of cottonwoods along Lightning Creek. The wide metal edge of the flatbed that served as a bumper was plastered with stickers of decidedly liberal causes, everything from gay rights to paid maternity leave, an unusually iconoclastic set of political beliefs for that isolated area of northeastern Oregon.

According to the USGS map I consulted earlier, the trail to his cabin wound five miles, crossing several fords that I soon discovered required a degree of heroics on the part of my little truck, over whose hood the current washed. The river cobbles slipped away beneath the tires, and I thought for sure that the truck would founder, the headlights glowing vaguely under green water. Meanwhile, lightning flashed overhead and thunder exploded with such concussive force it gave substance to the air, its echo repeating for miles. In the silence before the next strike came the sound of rocks skating down basalt cliffs in the nearby dark.

I pitched my tent far from the canyon walls across the meadow near the creek and joined Richard on the porch of the cabin, where we shared a flask as the rain poured then abruptly stopped, leaving just the sound of water dripping from leaves and the ambient song of the creek. When I asked, Richard said his return to the landscape of childhood seventy years ago was prompted "by worrisome little messages. Warnings."

I didn't know what he meant.

"Sometimes we get a little too serious for our own good," he said. "What you discover when you return to your place of origin," he said, "if there is anything such as an intact place to return to, you figure out pretty quickly that—" And here he trailed off without finishing his thought.

The singular fact about Lightning Creek is that there are no people. There's little evidence of occupation besides sporadic arrivals and departures: cattle drives in spring and fall, a few wanderers appearing on three-day holiday weekends in summer, fewer and fewer hunters as the season turns toward winter and the country above shuts down. The intimacies of Richard's childhood, all that seemed permanent then—the open-endedness of time, his parents and their friends following herds and harvests—appeared scarce now, seventy years on.

What we imagine we will find, we fail to find, but that isn't the same as saying it does not exist. In his poem "Bashō," the Dutch writer Cees Nooteboom observed once that "what vanished is still there as something that vanished." And that was largely borne out by Richard's experience.

The next morning, under strikingly calm, clear skies, he and I stood in the glistening meadow beside Lightning Creek. We lit a fire in a ring of stones and boiled water for tea.

Following his service in the Navy during the Korean War, Richard finished college, then lived aimlessly until, during the Kennedy administration, he joined the Peace Corps. After several years in Africa, he "pursued a career"—a vagueness that seemed intended as a judgment of the pursuit. He retired at the first opportunity, and then, his blood cells presenting some abnormalities, he hired on as a ranch hand in Lightning Creek, where his own parents had worked as hired hands when they were young. He was born nearby in 1926. He told me that he would probably die in the cabin behind us.

The Imnaha Canyon is one of those few places that remains more or less as it was a lifetime ago. The paved road, electricity, and phone didn't arrive anywhere in the canyon until well into the second half of the twentieth century and had still not arrived at Richard's cabin. That canyon was among the last places in the contiguous United States to enter the modern era, as we commonly think of it—the age of displacement, rootlessness, and loss. As such, there is still a recognizable place to return to there, a past seen, albeit through a liminal scrim.

Over black tea, Richard asked if I had noticed the tall ponderosa on the hillside at the canyon's mouth. "It's the tree Chief Joseph used to orient his retreat from General Howard's army. They began their war here. That tree marked the way across a low point in the ridge to Dug Bar. That's where he got his people across the river holding onto the manes of their horses as they swam. I imagine it was a somber crossing. They were leaving this country and must have wondered if they would ever see it again."

After a long pause, Richard looked up, a little surprised at his emotion. He laughed and pointed out that when Howard arrived, it took him three days to move his army across the same place in the river. "I think that tree is really not the original, though everyone wishes it were. And it could be, I suppose."

We sat in silence again for several more minutes while an azure bunting sang near the creek. Otherwise, the morning remained still. When he spoke again, he was still thinking about the Nez Perce retreat from eastern Oregon to Bear Paw, Montana. "So much happened after Joseph crossed that river. A lot of it sorrowful. You can't discount any of it. I mean, it didn't happen during my life, and the Nez Perce moved on well before my own parents came into this canyon. But it's never really over. The same is true about the camp of Chinese miners above Dug Bar, murdered for gold. That one seems a little more connected to the world I grew up in. When I was a kid, I knew who the murderers were. I'd see them in the summer up at the Grange. But either way, what happened here doesn't go away, and no matter how isolated this place seems, it played its role."

He went on to say that he had come to prefer the idea that the pine tree isn't the same tree because people are too often motivated by a longing to keep things the same. "History inhabits us, even if we pretend we don't bear its burden. In this canyon that particular horizon is very narrow. The burden is always here. And that hasn't made it easy to come back."

If the big tree at the mouth of the canyon was the tree Joseph used to orient his strategic retreat from the corrupt finale of manifest destiny, you might be able to more easily ignore the fact that Joseph's body is buried beside a littered highway in Washington State far from his father's grave and his own Wallowa homeland. The tree's continued existence would seem a form of inviolate presence, the past persisting without the moral complications of exile. Richard sipped from his cup and I wasn't interested, really, in pointing any of this out. Joseph was born just over the ridge to the north. He wasn't as lucky as Richard. He and those who followed him from this canyon and across a series of battlefields in Idaho and Montana bore the real burden of history. We looked up at the gap on the rim of the canyon. His mother had gone to Enterprise months before Richard's birth. Soon after, his father, on horseback, carried him into the canyon in his arms, an infant passing into this life through that low point on the ridge.

"Spain Saddle," he said. "We came down bench after bench of deep grass into a side-canyon of the Imnaha, forded the river, and then made our way back up here, where everyone was waiting to greet me and my mother on her return. All those people who lived here then are gone. I'm the only one left now."

A shadow crossed his face like a bird passing between him and the sun. He teared up and apologized. "I don't think I can say any more about any of this now. I'm sorry. Coming back here at this point in my life has been a little overwhelming. The day-to-day here is very simple, but I don't feel that way. It's not as simple as a routine." He poked the fire and then stared at the canyon walls directly above where we stood. His dilemma was clear and the waves of emotion he felt not so hopeful: "I'm here and can see it," he said referring to the community that occupied the canyon of his youth. "And yet I can see it's all gone, except inside of me." Simply re-inhabiting the canyon in no way guaranteed the past that was dear to him could reveal itself, much less endure beyond his life and into the lives and words of others.

⌁

Cartographers dispute whether Matterhorn Peak at 9,845 feet is the highest peak in the Eagle Cap Wilderness. Older maps indicate that Sacajewea Peak, just to the north of the Matterhorn, across a narrow, one-mile traverse, is a few feet higher. The two names, the two peaks, are emblems of the freakishness of American memory, and each is fatal in its way: the memorializing of indigenous claims now in exile; the mistaken notion that northeastern Oregon was merely a reflection of the European past.

During my first ascent of the Matterhorn, I was less concerned with elevations than the distance of my one-day, twenty-mile round trip. At the time I attempted that initial climb, the length and duration of the ordeal was expressive of some kind of youthful virtue. The "narrow, sandy ledges," however, that a far more experienced climber had described as an indication that the summit was in sight, seemed horribly exposed and soon enough caused me to abandon any vanity about virtuous ordeals.

The peak, it turned out, is more of a gently rounded ridge than the image suggested by the mountain's famous Swiss namesake.

From the east, the Oregon Matterhorn rises from Ice Lake into a mile-long, moderately steep wall. You would never mistake this Matterhorn for the iconic one above Zermatt. Still, the west face rising from Hurricane Creek is a five-thousand-foot vertical wall of poorly metamorphosed limestone, and even climbing from the east and peering from the summit over the west face into that abyss, one is aware of the heroics of Whymper on a barren crag. The climb so unnerved me, despite the appearance of the sandy ledges that simplified the final ascent and the broad, gentle aspect of the mountaintop, that I almost resigned from the climb just a few feet shy of the summit.

This pattern of behavior is characteristic of my admittedly modest experience as a mountaineer. Even today, after years of climbing with experienced rock and ice climbers whose cooing confidence has coaxed me up rock faces and over crags that seemed unclimbable, much less easy, I still lose nerve. There is a crucial transitional moment while ascending when it seems that one is ascending into air only, that the earth has given way above, and one must climb, as it were, blindly into the void. Gravity seems to weaken. Timidly looking behind me, that is, *down*, I find myself stymied by the appearance of nothing much above or below, only the immediate fact of the rock to which I cling. I lose my ability to focus my mind, and vertigo spirals through me like a worm.

At such moments of crisis, a lecture erupts inside my head on what we might call the natural history of human will. So as not to second-guess, as on that August day climbing the Matterhorn for the first time, I force myself to make one more inevitably simple but cautious move along the rock face and find myself standing on top of the mountain. That others virtually *walk* the same route is something to discuss another day.

Of that day almost twenty years ago, there appears only this brief entry in my journal: "Climbed Matterhorn today," and then, aside, and a little cryptically, "—the note left on the mountain." Of the first part of that fragmentary entry there is little to dispute. I climbed the mountain (admittedly not bravely) and recorded the fact in both my journal and in the shiny metal box the climbing club, the Mazamas, placed on the mountaintop.

Inside that box were messages, accumulated over a number of years, from climbers who had preceded me. One often finds in mountain records prose that is as predictable as the sunny summer days that inspired the words. Sealed jars or ammo boxes stuffed full of sentiments that express an anodyne Christianity, the pagan splendors of the "natural world," dharma bum I'm-living-in-the-moment bliss, and the you'd-have-to-be-one-to-understand the writer's *Übermensch* penetration of reality. All express an equal belief in their accomplished virtue.

But I know, or have convinced myself I know, that the note referred to in my journal was written by someone other than myself. On October 7, 1998, I tried to reconstruct the note, written by a recent retiree, that I failed to record verbatim on August 30, 1995:

> I was born here but moved away when I turned twelve and
> have lived the remainder of my life—another fifty years—at a
> great distance from these mountains. And now, near the end,
> I've come back to climb—while I can still climb—into the
> heart of the country I couldn't locate, even in memory. I'm
> happy, having found at last what eluded me all my life.

The false notes in this reconstruction are many and obvious. No one would have left such a note on the mountain. The intensifier "great" seems especially egregious. The two asides set off by dashes are an effort to describe what was perhaps only implied in the actual note. Worse yet, the phrase, "the heart of the country," is an obvious literary ornament borrowed from William Gass. The verb "locate" has more than a whiff of academic jargon and therefore disingenuousness. There was a note, however, left on that mountain, and that note, not my version of it, must have seemed genuine, and powerfully so, as it expressed the dilemma of not having entirely lived one's life as one might have chosen to live it—those past losses continuing to inflect the present.

Other references to this note occur on eight different dates between the second of December 2, 1998, and the December 12, 2001, by which time it had become a full-blown melodrama:

> She gave my brother life and died in spring, when a small
> band of Nez Perce still returned to dig camas in the swales
> of my father's meadow—the mirage of abundance. The year
> I turned twelve we moved farther west, and I have lived a
> lifetime at a great distance from these mountains, doing work
> I despise among people I can't love or leave. I have come back
> only to climb for this one day, while I can still climb to the
> core of what memory concocted, possibly a cruel device, this
> landscape I partly invented: ribbons of glittering snowmelt,
> forested canyons, knife-edged ridges of marble, seven glacial
> lakes milky with silt and ice, a dome of careless sky. This sin-
> gular, dizzying pleasure: vertigo whirling from groin to brain.
> And now, to have lived long enough to stand here at last,
> almost worthy of the penalty of being born.

Obviously, things have gotten out of hand. Whatever the actual note on the mountain said is completely obscured in clouds of mythopoesis, evidence of my failure to imagine the actual circumstances of another man's life, his birth cry of the universe substituted with a fantasy. Whoever that older man was who wrote the original note on the mountain, the message had been lost. He seems vague and inaccessible now, slipping back through borderlands of what memory concocted. And yes, perhaps *that* is a cruel device.

Since that morning in 1995, I've climbed the Matterhorn no fewer than a half-dozen times, and once or twice without trepidation on the "narrow, sandy ledges." On all subsequent climbs, I've searched the mountaintop for that box the Mazamas placed there, hoping to find the actual note left by the man who lived his life separated from the place that claimed him at birth. Despite being told that the box is there, those searches in the rocks piled on the summit and in protected crevasses proved pointless. Like the birth cry of the universe I heard once, like my suicidal friend Moritz and melancholy Richard's childhood acquaintances, like all the lost worlds we wait to re-inhabit us, the Mazamas box and the note it contained have gone missing.

THE OLD MARRIAGE

Walking home one autumn afternoon years ago, when we first moved to Oregon and our children were still children, I passed a neighbor's house, on the tiny front porch of which her aged parents sat in chairs in the sun. They were a very old couple, though how old I can't say. They seemed like ancients. The old woman was senile, oblivious and silent, the disconnections in her mind a vast *terra incognita*. He, almost blind, seemed aware of his life and the world around him. They were so weak and frail neither could move from their chairs without assistance. As I passed by that warm afternoon, I watched the old man lift his hand from under the plaid blanket on his lap and reach blindly into the space between them, groping for her hand that hung limp beside the armrest of her chair.

❧

Evenings in dismal January, when we believe that our sojourn in La Grande is nearing its end, we begin inviting friends for long dinners. These formal evenings have proven effective for coping with a chronic lack of purpose we've felt since the departure of our children for their adult lives. We hadn't anticipated any

113

loss of that reliable, future-oriented focus that is launching one's children into the world. At times since we've felt with growing awareness that nature is done with us. We've fulfilled all it asks really, and we find ourselves adrift and increasingly melancholy as winter deepens. By January 2005, we'd been granted our private lives again after twenty years, but this privacy was like heavy coats we'd checked in the cloak room before entering a concert of garish band tunes. The performance had ended, and what a performance it was! Once we exited the concert hall, though, it seemed we'd been given some other couple's ill-fitting and strange coats by mistake. Even worse, try as we may, we couldn't get the loud and familiar melodies of those martial tunes out of our heads.

One evening after dinner, we emptied the remainder of the wine into our glasses, and one of our guests asked, "Is it possible to give a proper eulogy for a couple who have loved longer than you have lived?"

"I beg your pardon?" Josefa asked for us both.

"Our parents," our guest from the city said. "How, for example, would we eulogize them?" She paused to wait for an answer, and though no one had laughed, she interrupted our silence to say, "Don't laugh, I'm totally sincere about this."

"Your parents are still alive," I said.

"Put it this way," she went on. "How would you go about ensuring you received a proper eulogy, after a long marriage? What kind of guarantee can there be?"

"None?" I said.

Perhaps there was something else to consider, perhaps even a contrary argument to make, though I could think of none. We'd poised at the threshold of bringing the evening to a close, and now we were going to have to choose whether to go on past midnight. We sat there, frowning at our wine glasses, waiting for someone to decide. "Would anyone like more pie?" I said, then rose, went into the kitchen, and soon returned with seconds of huckleberry pie and a bottle of port.

Evening comes early in January, lasts long, and ends in a small dawn that enacts itself over several brave but bleak hours behind the high foothills to the southeast, where windmills tower and churn the air above the wind-glazed snow of Pyle Canyon. Only a small lamp burned in a far corner of the room, and besides the light of the fire in the woodstove in the opposite corner and the guttering candles burned down to stubs, the room remained in shadow. The rose-colored walls glowed like the light I have long imagined is the light that comforts us in the womb. Most evenings during winter passed with us hunkered down in chairs, reading, listening to music, the walls glowing, as though our solitude were a long-sought-after consolation. Some evenings I would look up at the end of the Haydn cello concerto and feel that I might cry, but whether because an enlightened age of man had or hadn't arrived, I couldn't say.

Our guests and conversation aside, the intimate consolations were no different on this evening than on those nights just the two of us shared these rooms. Swirls of falling snow ghosted across windowpanes. A fugitive draft stirred the curtains and gently lifted the leaves of house plants. One voice in the shadowy room, the sister of our friend, said, "Too much of a young couple's life is taken up with the demands nature makes upon them. Few can resist that. And why should they? It either happens before we're mature enough to think about it, or it fails to happen at all. For me, it ended in failure, it never happened at all."

This we greeted with silence, though what she said we agreed was true. A young couple is so distracted by their immediate, pointed desires and the need to satisfy them that to act rationally at a young age, to think or to plan, seems *contra naturam*. That was our experience anyway. The events of our lives unfolded beyond our power to control them. Every day seemed to test our capacity for wonder. Whatever skills we possessed that might enable our survival seemed newly discovered and, at best, provisional.

Our friends explained that their parents had recently retired and were planning their funerals. This worried their daughters, who imagined the actual funerals would be dismal, directed by pushy, garish aunts and uncles. In no way would anything their parents or their parents' siblings planned reflect the fullness of the lives being eulogized. The quality of love their parents expressed for one another existed in an efficient language of gestures their daughters couldn't exactly decode. It was a language so intimate it seemed their parents often communicated silently. One can almost put aside the obvious achievements of a lifetime, I understood the sisters to be saying, because achievements are after all too few and transitory, moments that fail to reflect the reality of ordinary life. We ought to prefer the greater consolations of the mundane, all that time spent cutting up onions with tears in our eyes, boiling water for coffee, doing dishes, folding laundry, drawing a bath, backing the car down the drive, weeding the garden, what we always are doing, and more often than not, doing in silence.

The sisters felt they couldn't elaborate on what would reflect the genuine qualities of the life their parents shared, over fifty years—thirty since *they* left their parents' house. "If you think of it in those terms," one sister said, "we make the greatest claims on them, though we've been less a part of their lives than we imagine. And their siblings even more so, scattered and estranged from daily life. Their closest friends know them better than anyone else, but few of them will outlive our parents."

There are times I can no more grasp the dimensions of intimacy for the long married than those who are presumably less lucky or lost their chance. Opportunities for any true feeling of intimacy are so few. I remember, though, coming upon an accident in the ice fog before dawn west of Pendleton, Oregon. It was almost as crazily stupid to stop on the shoulder of the road as it was simply to be out on that road at all, at that hour and in those conditions. An SUV was sprawled on its side in the snowy median, vulnerable and strange, out of place, even a little indecent. Its contents had scattered, doors flying open and glass shattering as it rolled. I hesitated, but then stopped and rushed to the victim, who staggered toward me through icy fog and deep snow. We embraced, and he asked, "*¿Estoy vivo?*" I assured him we were both very much alive and we began laughing, then embraced, kissing each other on both cheeks. We're still alive!

The births of my children aside, I don't think I have ever felt happier about mortality and intimacy than in that moment. The accident victim was an undocumented immigrant on his way to work in his friend's vehicle. That the accident was a colossally unfortunate complication goes without saying. He called his friend, who said not to worry, he'd take care of it. How it all worked out, I don't know. I simply drove him to work. Somehow, he arrived on time.

I poured our guests another glass of port. All we can ever offer each other is the assurance: "You are not alone." And perhaps this, too: "I will not betray you."

~⋄~

The following morning, I was still wondering what is a proper eulogy? Why should the parents of our friends risk any inauthentic speechifying such as the professionals of death rush to the pulpit or graveside to deliver? Or worse, convenience and one's exhaustion aside, why should the grief-stricken (or the deceased, for that matter) agree to such an abomination as the professional insincerity of those for whom our lives and our deaths are merely an opportunity to exercise a practiced skill for pay? That's big talk and reason enough to prefer the gravediggers seated on their backhoe, not quite decently out of sight or mind, as they smoke and chat at the periphery of someone else's grief.

After a month in her deathbed, awaiting the sentence she didn't fear being carried out, an elderly neighbor and friend died in her sleep late one Saturday night. At noon the following Wednesday, somber December light filling the Methodist sanctuary, where she lay before us in her coffin. As we sat in the dark walnut pews in a half-circle around her, each indicted by his or her careless life, the skin on my forearms and nape prickled, as though her spirit had just brushed past. But then the lay minister stumbled through the eulogy, and I felt ashamed by what he had asked her husband and children to reveal in the family interview. Why would anyone condescend to my deceased friend Roberta, as the minister seemed to be doing, as baffled as her family by the woman I thought I knew? Why laugh at her now, why call her "eccentric," who in the last act of her life demanded her freedom from a place as narrow as the eye of a needle others had threaded for her?

She had been an ordinary young woman at a time when leaving the house would have been a betrayal of every expectation others placed on her, in her role as mother and wife. Even at the moment of her passing from our lives, no one seemed curious about, much less willing to acknowledge, the principled public figure she became. Only when we sang, "He leadeth me beside still waters," did I feel the spirit moving again in my chest, and then again, hours later, skiing up the canyon where I often found her, when she was a very old woman and already gravely ill, hands behind her back, head bowed, lost in her thoughts, walking alone in the forest. A limb brushed my shoulder. When I turned, there was no one there, only the low, December sun, distant on its curve in the south, broken clouds igniting before the sky faded toward violet dusk.

⌁

In her poem "Our Ancestor's Short Lives," the Polish poet Wisława Szymborska asserts that in the past, "Old age was the privilege of rocks and trees." Accordingly, neither Roberta nor I, who were separated in age by forty years or more, would have lived so long as to become acquainted. Earlier generations, entangled in the demands of nature, matured, reproduced, and vanished soon after: "they are yet," Szymborska says, "And then they are gone. / Infinity's ends fused quickly."

The morning's newspapers recently printed a photo of two skeletons facing each other. We understand the implicit intention of the pose. Their legs are drawn up as though they kneeled together to embrace with their deracinated arms. Each smiles into the other's empty eye sockets. It's the ghastly smile of Death's head and its perfect teeth, but their teeth *are* perfect because this couple died young. Archeologists will test the age of their bones and artifacts buried with them, but believe the burial occurred as long ago as six thousand years in what is now the city of Mantua. The name of that city alone evokes an improbable, albeit sympathetic answer to the unanswerable question of their identities and why those who knew and presumably loved them buried this couple in such a way as to honor their intimacy. Here is act V, and the unwritten scene 4 of *Romeo and Juliet*: this pose preserved for eternity, or a nearly so.

This couple has little to do with Shakespeare or any of his sources; rather, they more certainly echo John Berger, for whom the image of the place of his burial with the beloved is consolation enough for the inevitability of death. It's a burial that is hardly burial at all, but a random casting of the lovers' bones upon the earth that, whether discovered or not, and whether others recognize it or not, is the consolation of having loved. When he concludes this reverie, Berger says to his beloved: "with you I can imagine a place where to be phosphate of calcium is enough." I can't say I entirely believe him or would believe myself were I to make such a claim. Besides, the ritualized burial of the young couple in Mantua seems more resonantly and deliberately eloquent, perhaps of other greater, more hopeful and durable human wishes than Berger's celebratory acquiescence to nature. Berger likely would disagree on that point because, according to his view, to return to earth with one's beloved as one of the essential chemical elements of life (and to be light-emitting!) is to form a more literal bond with the beloved than loving-making itself, or even a child born of that loving-making. Here is an ultimate interpenetration of being in the near-eternity of the periodic table.

᠃

I once had a student, a man my own age as it happened, and a native of this valley, long married to a nurse who supported him as he fumbled affably from the Army, where he was a large truck mechanic, to the railroad, where he was a brakeman, to layoffs, and finally in his early forties to university and a degree in primary education. Although we weren't friends, I shared a more casual acquaintance with him than with his classmates. Both of us having grown up in the 1960s, our assumption was that we understood one another well enough. We could make the usual conversation about where we were when the Kennedys and King were assassinated, or when *Sgt. Pepper's* was released, or share a memory of a life-sized black and white poster of Rachel Welch in hip-huggers and a bikini top, or the first time we smoked oregano or corn silk, and then the first time we smoked pot or dropped acid while listening to Ummagumma or the guitar solo in "Machine Gun." The afternoon of Nixon's resignation speech found us both listening (three time zones apart on opposite sides of the nation) to tiny AM transistor radios.

I don't remember my student's name, though I remember it was the early 1990s and he still wore a mullet and photochromic glasses. Still, I felt affection for him whenever he appeared at my office door, as he did one day at the end of winter term. He was distraught, his face ashen, his eyes red-rimmed from crying, all his easy bluster deflated. He told me his wife had just died in her sleep at home the night before last. *Of natural causes*, he emphasized. I thought nothing of it at the time, but this last detail seemed in retrospect a point of doubt. He told me he would not be in school for the remainder of the term, would I please give him an incomplete instead of an F, and would I please come to her funeral. "That," he said, "would mean a lot to me." I didn't know his wife and can't say with any certainty that I even knew he *had* a wife until that moment.

Besides Josefa, seated next to me, I knew no one at the funeral but my student, who sat in a metal folding chair in the front row, stock-still in his ill-fitting suit. He seemed to have recovered and was now traveling that dull, mud-flat world that follows shocking news. The chapel was a narrow, curtained room aglow with soft natural light, the source of which were skylights. The funeral director greeted everyone at the door with the practiced and well-oiled solemnity of any undertaker.

By the time we reached the eulogy, the minister who conducted the service admitted that neither the deceased nor her spouse were members of his church; rather they were people with whom he had grown up, and that he had asked to give this eulogy for one from whom he long had been estranged, spiritually and socially. It was an unusually frank admission. I gasped a little at the thought that my student had agreed to this. Beyond that, I remember thinking, all the way through his remarks, how well he knew this couple. La Grande is a very small town, even smaller for those who are natives and never moved away. They were each a part of the others' lives, and not only in their own generation; in their parents' and grandparents' generations, they had lived in the same neighborhoods and worked in the same mills. True, he admitted, their participation in each other's daily life was ultimately peripheral, someone once close in childhood, to whom as an adult you expressed the usual pleasantries whenever you met in the street, and then observed from a distance that couldn't be bridged, because you had become devout and they had rejected all that. Besides noting the different paths their lives had followed, he discreetly avoided that subject as morally not otherwise instructive.

I felt as stirred by the man's candor as I was by Psalm 23 at Roberta's funeral. He implied no sanction with this simple statement of facts; that is, he carefully avoided any Christian sanctimony about salvation in Jesus and eternal life in a resort holiday of heaven. He seemed a serious enough man to recognize that hope and immortality were secure only in memory, and memory is as fragile as life itself. Speaking in this manner, he remained entirely close to her life as he knew it, and all the goodness and humanity that he could reveal there, principally, that she had spent her entire adult life nursing others. Then he sang, sotto voce, what her husband had confided to him was her favorite song, a hymn from her childhood, "Softly and Tenderly," the implication being that she had put into action a care that others, often more pious than herself, merely professed. I left that chapel shaken by the loss of a life I hadn't known and by the necessity to make provision for others in memory, to give attention to that portion of other lives that remains largely unnoticed and possibly unknowable.

Later, I mentioned all of this to friends, nurse-practitioners, both of whom I imagined knew my student's spouse professionally, and each responded, "Oh, her. She was a suicide. Stole the drugs. She knew which ones would do the go-to-bed-and-wake-up-dead trick."

The matter-of-fact gallows humor probably should not have surprised me, but at least I understood then what had been at stake for my student when he insisted his wife had died in her sleep of natural causes. I understood how the minister's discretion was much greater even than I imagined.

❧

News arrived not long ago of a double drowning in Montana's Flathead Lake in January: an older couple we'd known since our student days, one of them my reluctant mentor, whose influence on my life was, to use the term he loved and borrowed from James Joyce, *ineluctable*. They owned a cabin on Wildhorse Island, where we visited them many years ago not long after they began staying there during their holidays. I remember the island being a mile or so from the marina on the southern shore of the lake. H— told Josefa, during what would be our only visit there, that he and N— sometimes canoed to and from the island in winter, though they only did so when circumstances forced them to, and then took every precaution. "They aren't risk-averse people," Josefa told me later.

This winter they crossed to the island in their powerboat. They stayed for a few days, but as N— had scheduled a flight to Los Angeles to visit her aging father, they intended to return to shore and drive to the airport. Apparently, the powerboat would not start. They did what they had done before, what H— had assured they accomplished with due diligence: they began canoeing across that short stretch of open water. They never made it, though no one knows why their canoe capsized. They wore life jackets, but not survival suits, so hypothermia quickly killed them. They were found days later, together, floating near the island, their dogs howling from shore.

Reading their eulogies in the local newspaper, I was baffled by what I read about my older friends whose lives ceased to be, in any meaningful sense, a part of my own daily life more than twenty years ago. The honorifics of university professor and accountant fell woefully short of describing the two longtime Missoula residents "whose unexpected deaths rocked a huge community of friends," as the article begins.

One friend described my mentor as a scholar of James Joyce who also mastered sailboat design, small-engine repair, and poker.

Another said the people who knew N— as someone who could midwife a troubled ewe probably didn't know she also had one of the top scores in the nation when she took the certified public accountant's exam. The pair rode their motorcycles across much of the globe. In eulogizing H— at Saturday afternoon's memorial service, yet another friend recalled Joyce's claim from "The Dead" that it's better to die pursuing a passion than to have never lived. What magnifies their deaths is the way they lived their lives, he said. H— could run a garage sale with the skill of a Chicago commodities broker and his musical taste ran from Yo-Yo Ma to Neil Diamond. A fellow accountant at N—'s firm said she decided to take up accounting in midlife because in accounting there are only right and wrong answers. N— decided to take up cross-country motorcycling as a natural expression of her sense of adventure.

All agreed that Joyce's Bloomsday celebration on June sixteenth was a good day to remember the couple as well. "Conjure up a vision of both of them in their fringed leathers," one friend said, "just chasing their shadows, heading east." Besides agreeing about the Bloomsday celebration, or better yet, declaring on that date the arrival on earth of the too-long-delayed New Bloomusalem, my first response to all this was to think how little I really knew my mentor and his wife. I'm certain the intentions of their friends were kind and generous, and surely these people were more intimate with them than we were, but something about it seemed cloying. Perhaps it's the reference to "The Dead" that misjudges the story.

Say whatever you like, but should we really model our lives on the actions of a seventeen-year-old who catches his death of rain and cold? Maybe. I remember, though, that my teacher dwelled longer over the final passages of *Ulysses* than "The Dead." There, Molly Bloom welcomes Leopold into their bed again after his long day's journey haunted by the ghost of their son, and recalls embracing Leopold for the first time: ". . . and then he asked me would I yes to say yes my mountain flower and first I put my arms around him yes and drew him down to me so he could feel my breasts all perfume yes and his heart was going like mad and yes I said yes I will Yes."

For years, I wished to return to Montana, to Talking Water Creek, a small tributary to Flathead Lake, where my real life began when I married a foreign-looking girl. That return has never come, and despite occasional visits, we never surpassed the borderlands of our fatalism until late one winter afternoon, when we were skiing along a trail in the Wallowa Mountains near Salt Creek Summit and looked out across Hell's Canyon eastward to the Seven Devils and the Idaho massif, on the far eastern edge of which the mountains descend into Montana. We could see it there. Almost. I permitted myself the privilege, anyway, of imagining that we could see it, where violet demarcated the onset of twilight. I felt a moment's amnesty from the little injuries that salted my blood with shame. Shame at the fact that we knew we'd failed to find our way back to the life we began there, years before we came to Oregon; shame because we might never return but remain always an absence among those other lives we imagined went on, happier and more successful than ours, like H—'s and N—'s, whose lives we were a part of once. Shame for the Michael Furey–like delusion that we'd lost something we couldn't recover. We returned, not to Montana, but to a grove in our minds, our own Bloomusalem, under a high canopy of ponderosas, dry snow stirring into whirlwinds, the heavy boughs swaying, and the entire landscape falling silent as the sky's granite edge.

We looked back toward the north, the direction our lives were heading, briefly, half a lifetime earlier, when we changed course. It was years since we seemed right. Almost at ease. That low angle of sun on our faces. Snow dazzling us with its acclaim. The circumstances of poverty had insisted that we abandon the first vow we swore. We traveled together nearly thirty years, and then, moving ahead another thirty in our minds, leaving the makeshift cabin at the edge of Montana hayfields, followed weedy, infinitely branching trails, labored in the weather of meanness and loss. We made a second vow to chance, to join our ashes there at the end, at Talking Water Creek, our phosphate of calcium sifting into the place we never intended to stray from—a permanent household of bear grass, of lupine, and balsamroot, the voice of that stream talking its fractaled way to the lake where our unlucky friends drowned.

The terror of that moment the canoe capsized is what goes on haunting our private thoughts. Tonight, we try to measure our own response in these appalling circumstances. The agonizing likelihood of our recovering for a moment, finding one another in the freezing water, thinking that maybe we can survive this, and then knowing we can't. It's a moment we aren't usually permitted to observe others suffer, an unspeakable extremity of human intimacy and vulnerability. If there is any wisdom in it for those about to die, it's beyond our knowing. We can only hope that when it comes, it resonates peace, the truest eulogy.

SOMETIMES THE GREAT DEPRESSION

Autumn is the time of year for combating my melancholy with the making of a proper soup.

On weekends in the 1960s cold and dreary as today, I played outdoors from first light to dusk. Without siblings or friends close by in the neighborhood of older factory workers like my grandparents, I spent those long days alone imagining whatever I pleased. A favorite dream was to "step-off" the distance in yards around my grandparents' house, front and back, and multiply it by as many times as necessary to equal a whole series of track events, including the thirty-six-lap mile, in which I went head to head (in my head) against the legendary miler Jim Ryan. I made a long jump on the sidewalk in the side yard. A high-jump pit in the maple leaves. Two sawhorses for the intermediate hurdles. And just so, I spent the day competing against myself in track and field events, Howard Cosell providing his color commentary on the drama unfolding around my grandparents' post-war Cape cottage.

On the rare weekend day when my grandfather worked overtime on Saturday, my grandmother called me in at dusk for a bowl of soup. She called it beef barley soup, though you would not mistake it for anything other than vegetable beef soup. For this soup she always used an electric skillet rather than her usual cast iron Dutch oven that I use today to prepare a similar recipe. Perhaps this was because she made such a limited quantity—just one large serving really, for me, her ex post facto son, who still smelled of the cold air and fallen leaves. Her beef barley soup was a gift whose meaning was rooted deep in her past, and that she intended only for me. There might also be a loaf of fresh bread cooling on wire racks, and she would be making freshly cooked applesauce for dessert. When I came in the door, the back porch and kitchen smelled of sautéed ground beef and onions, peeled potatoes, plumped out barley, and salty stewed tomatoes. Just before serving, she added peas, corn, a chopped carrot and a chopped stalk of celery. Then she did something truly extravagant for her: she opened the cupboard, reached for a bottle of Worcestershire Sauce, and splashed in a few drops.

I thought it possibly the finest soup ever made. Better than the won ton soup at the Teahouse in Akron. Better even than the fresh chicken noodle soup the old women in their cotton print farm dresses served every summer at the Fairmont Grange. *That* soup was remarkable for its homemade egg noodles and home-grown chicken, with golden coins of fat floating on top. My favorite, though, was the far more robust beef barley soup served on those cold, damp, autumn days. For years after I left home and was living on a tight budget, I alternated every other week making either chili or my grandmother's soup in such quantities as to be able to eat it every day for a week at a time. On special occasions, I made it for my friends at university. Once before she died, when she found herself stranded in my apartment after a blizzard, I made her beef barley soup, and it pleased her. She could barely suppress her smile, much less hood the pleasure that glistened in her eyes, though otherwise she was outwardly as stoic and undemonstrative as anyone who expected nothing much from life. And finally, I made the soup for my own children. At dusk on an autumn day, during which they spent their time outdoors much as I had decades earlier, I would call them indoors, where they were greeted by that same savory aroma that greeted me in the 1960s, and, I presume, my mother in the 1940s, perhaps even my grandmother herself before her mother's early exit from life.

All of which I'm thinking about today as I, older than my grandmother was when she first made me beef barley soup, gather up what is left out here in the garden. Fifty years later and living in this isolated valley on the western edge of the Rockies, it's still easy to slip back to Ohio in the 1960s, to the deep solitude of my childhood after my father died. Soon after his death my young mother seemed like more of an absence than a presence. Her parents, who carried the scarcities and bleakness of the Great Depression into every aspect of their lives, tried their best to bolster a boy shaken badly by circumstances.

Her soup is still the gift of all of that.

～❧

By late October the garden I sowed eight months ago is mostly kaput. Three nights of hard frost and everything that wasn't cold hardy has turned flaccid, collapsed, and begun to deliquesce. It's time to gather up the few remaining vegetables from the beds and make that honored pot of soup.

What is left in the garden to make this soup? My inventory so far: a flat of very ripe Romas, a bowl of misshapen green and yellow wax beans, a couple sprouting shallots missed when I dug them up months ago, green onions, several pencil-thin summer squash, a bunch of sweet carrots, two slug-bejeweled potatoes that surfaced after I turned over the bed and hauled away a bushel of russets in September, a woody stalk of basil burned browned along the edges of its leaves by frost, and sprigs of rosemary from a plant I must dig up, pot, and bring inside for the winter. It all lies there arranged on the backdoor stoop, glistening in a light, chilly rain.

Those are enough ingredients for soup tonight and possibly tomorrow.

And there is more here to harvest that will go into other soups later in the season, like the big globes of beets and whatever kale has not become infested with aphids that will go into the borscht whose recipe comes to us from a German student who made it for us decades ago. The kale, though, is very much in doubt. The swarms of ladybugs we released into the garden in the spring and that tended to the garden's well-being have crawled into crannies in the rock wall for the duration, along with those industrious, self-sacrificing aphid farmers, the ants; thus the aphids cluster unmolested and very unappetizingly around the stalks of the otherwise broad, blue, ruffled leaves of kale. But beet greens are of no interest to aphids and are a good enough substitute for kale. We will leave in the ground the aromatic leeks for potato soup, the soup one serves to cure winter's colds or influenza: "The potato," my grandmother claimed in one of her peculiar idioms, "absorbs away germs." At first sign of "peakedness" she had once sent my childhood self to bed and brought me a bowl of her cure-all, having felt my forehead with the back of her hand and determined that my fever hadn't yet broken and must therefore be fed.

We've made one additional, hopeful gesture to the near future: on the floor of the greenhouse and inside the cold frame tucked into the rock wall, Josefa and I have sown a dozen different varieties of red, green, and dappled lettuce, chard, mustard and collards, and these have all popped up out of the soil, their seedlings already swaying toward the faint urgency of sunlight that barely lifts itself above the mountain ridge to the south—on the rare day, that is, when the sky is actually clear. But who do I think I'm kidding? It's a rainy 9 a.m. on a Saturday in autumn and it seems no lighter now than it did two hours ago when I came outside in the dreary dawn. Even if it were clear, the sun would soon pass at a low angle over the garden in a matter of hours. Long shadows would lie across everything. What we planted in the greenhouse isn't likely to thrive, much less live long, and even now its sweetness is turning bitter. Maybe there is a month yet to grow those hopeful greens under glass. By Thanksgiving, the last of it will have been eaten with gratitude, but only if we're lucky enough to avoid a prolonged cold.

December will arrive with the dark of the old year, and January will not provide much promise of a remedy to that dusky, cold world. Then maybe by late February if we're lucky, or April Fool's Day if we're not, what wants to go on living will resume its latent vigor, growing bright and tender again, the light as strong by then as it was a month ago, and sweetness will return to these plants under glass.

❧

Though our sons didn't know her well, and perhaps can't recall her brief presence in their lives, they nevertheless enjoyed their great-grandmother's soup as much as I did. Eventually, they requested the recipe, which I provide here verbatim: Beef makes the base of the broth. Whether it's ground or stew cut, you must sauté it in oil and black pepper, at the bottom of a stock pot. (If you have all day, use a soup bone; if not, vegetable bouillon). Add a pinch of summer savory, a sacred herb. Also add marjoram, thyme, and rosemary. For sweetness, a tablespoon of celery seed. Splash on Worcestershire Sauce (balsamic is okay), and be liberal with it, as it gives the broth its pleasing tartness. Peel and cut up chunky-style a few potatoes; likewise, a yellow onion. Stir these into the braised meat and reduce the heat. Pour in two pints of tomato juice canned the previous summer, but store bought stewed or fresh tomatoes are fine. The stockpot is maybe one-third full.

Meanwhile, begin cooking a cup of barley in a separate pot. Once the grains have fluffed, drain and set the barley aside. Let the broth simmer as quietly as time allows. Chop carrots and celery (winter squash and summer squash are good additions, too, as available). Put these aside with green peas and corn. Don't add these until the soup is almost ready to serve, or they will be reduced to a disgusting mush (I need not elaborate here on the gastronomic virtues of firm vegetables nor the ghastliness of overcooked ones). When the potatoes have softened, but haven't succumbed to mealiness, add the last vegetables, allowing them only to cook enough so they are tender and all other ingredients hot on the tongue.

This is the recipe born of a poverty that required generations to overcome. Though it resembles my grandmother's soup, mine is a richer soup than any my forebears believed possible, prudent or even moral. Serve this only with fresh baked brown, black, or sourdough bread, though I admit a weakness for Milton's Everything crackers. This soup, I explained to our sons, is enough to satisfy all but the bloodless aristocrat in them, which means that, should they ever deign to make and eat this soup, they will be fully satisfied, because they are not aristocrats in any conceivable sense of the word.

❧

A month ago, in late September, we still were eating our dinners in the garden at dusk, the shadows tiered above us in the treetops on the hillside. Crows cawed as they flew from all directions to their roosts. There was the occasional flutter of a sphinx moth hovering over geraniums. And one night, a loose group of nighthawks passed high above, dipping and rising erratically as they hunted. Another night a tiny speck of iridescent green perched on a telephone wire—a female rufous hummingbird at rest during her long migration to the Gulf Coast. As it grew darker, bats, silent and agile, passed like wraiths dodging through the evening air, fattening themselves for the long night, imminent by then, when their hearts would slow, their body temperatures drop, and they would stumble or crawl as in a dream toward shelter and a season of sleep.

I will soon stumble toward shelter, but there is this soup to make well before sleep, and there are still these tomato plants to uproot one at a time and drag like giant squid across the garden to toss into the pile I'll shred and add to the compost. I yank out the sunflowers, ropes of pickles and squash vines, zinnias, tomatillos (saving in a jar one of the lacy globes of the deracinated fruit for no reason other than my astonishment at the delicacy of the thing), woody basil, and dry bean pods attached to runners. The same with the tall marigolds planted between tomatoes. All of it goes into the pile to chop. There are still peonies to cut back, rotted rhubarb stems to pull, and both to cover in Rumpelstiltskin's straw.

By the time the parsley materializes in the corner, tucked up under the table grapes beside the greenhouse, rain has soaked me through to the skin. The wind's come up and the temperature is falling as the cold front passes and the snow level lowers into the foothills.

Where in God's name did all this parsley come from? How had it escaped notice?

The seed heads overhang six feet of garden path and dropped the infinitesimal seeds of Persephone's sacred herb every time we brushed past. The parsley means, that is, to take over the world, as well it should, or at least this little uncontested corner of it.

I high-grade the plants for tabouleh, a dish my grandmother would not have considered making, though perhaps she might have tried, if *Ladies' Home Journal*, *Redbook*, or *Good Housekeeping* had featured an exotic recipe for a Middle Eastern dinner circa 1970, with accompanying photos of the Shah of Iran's elegant wife, Farah Pahlavi, perhaps, very pleased to serve her family such humble fare. I'm certain that my grandmother had never heard of tabouleh, nor had she ever seen bulgur wheat for sale at Persky's Market on State Street. She once took a brief interest in East Indian cooking, however, probably a result of excited encouragement from one of those print repositories of modern domesticity: it was the absolute blandest curry possible. With sultanas (a true extravagance, really) sprinkled on top. There's nothing else to report about the East Indian dish she cooked and served my grandfather and me, the Grand Vizier and prince of her humble table, but I remember the great fuss she made about the spices. Where she purchased these, I can't even guess. Probably she made substitutions.

I chop the rest of the parsley back to the ground with the green-stained blade of the *kama*, heap it up, and am about to toss the rest of that sodden mess onto the compost pile, when, again, I reconsider.

All this parsley is so much more than what we need, and the compost prefers green. Yet as improbable a moral problem as this is, like many Americans, my tendency is toward a hyperbolic and apocalyptic imagination about the future. The Great Depression might return after all, as Prohibition might return. W. C. Fields, considering the latter possibility a reality, kept (according to no less reliable authority than Groucho Marx) an attic full of whiskey. "Why?" Groucho asked. "Prohibition ended years ago." "You never know," his friend Bill replied. "It might return." Alcohol never passed my grandmother's lips, but she and my grandfather communicated their fear of poverty, dispossession, and diaspora in every criticism of my spendthrift disposition, lack of self-discipline, and foolhardy belief that I could live above my class.

When the first credit cards arrived in the mail from Master-Card in 1966, they opened the envelope, gravely read the accompanying letter with their hands over their mouths, and instead of angrily destroying the objects of temptation (those plastic cards had the power of taboo in their minds, and to destroy them would have evoked an incalculably bad outcome), they hid the cards in the secret compartment of an old chest of drawers from which the cards never again emerged. When I asked why they hid the cards and never used them, they only shook their heads and said, obliquely, "They are very bad people who sent these to us." *They* were bankers, investors, speculators, the worst people on the planet, who already had once destroyed the only world my grandparents knew.

Waste not . . . a penny saved . . . a stitch in . . . all those proverbs of theirs are inside me still, shouting their singular claim. This parsley could prove more valuable than the heat it might still generate in the compost. My grandparents' view of the moral category of frugality wasn't at all unlike the one Donald Hall knew from his grandparents, who had a box in their New Hampshire attic labeled "string too short to be saved."

I bring out my great grandmother's scale, on which they weighed me after my birth. I sort through the parsley again, bundle it into bunches to give away. Piled into a bowl, the bunches all together weigh—well, it's hard to say because the numbers are worn from the scale, so I guess, maybe two pounds?

⌀

It's been like this every year for decades, centuries really: the dream of abundance accompanied by the fear of scarcity.

As a child, I wondered why my grandmother so scrupulously washed tin cans, removed the labels, folded the ends inside, and handed them over to my grandfather, who then meticulously crushed them with a sledge and arranged the flattened metal in an old repurposed tar bucket until it was full. He took it all away somewhere, to Kulka's or Hymie Munitz's scrapyards I supposed, where he would be rewarded for his virtue and respect for the scarcities of the past with—what?—fifty cents profit? This he would make a big deal about "investing in the Davy Fund," which paid for my shoes. They also saved old bread wrappers they washed out and dried. Hundreds of plastic bags. Nobody else we knew did this, not even people poorer than ourselves. At one point during my mother's lonely peregrinations through the ghettos of Akron and Canton, Ohio, she found herself working in a plastic bag factory, and on her occasional visits to Alliance she would bring us "seconds" from the factory. Thirty years later, cleaning out my grandmother's house, we would find these same sour-smelling bags, washed out, a little tacky to the touch with a film of congealed grease, but otherwise ready for use.

Had we not been released yet from the Great Depression? My grandparents kept in practice, just in case we were all called upon again to join in a common effort to save ourselves from the excesses and evils of others less chaste than ourselves. Their closets were packed with clothes from the 1920s, 30s, 40s, and 50s, all of which my grandmother methodically stitched into quilts or wove into rag rugs, or most ingenious of all, fashioned into wildly hideous hats she made for the ladies in her "circle," as she referred to them. Of the alterations she made to these old clothes, which constituted a good deal of my wardrobe well into my teens, the less said the better. Nothing was thrown away, ever. If we broke a garden tool, it was carefully repaired in the garage of a neighboring spot-welder. Blades were kept sharp, tools oiled, machines serviced and then protected in a thin layer of machine oil before being put away for winter.

In the spirit of the holidays, though, my grandmother would splurge by making sweet rolls and fresh-squeezed orange juice for breakfast. She always was careful when dividing the dough to make certain each sweet roll had one piece of walnut meat and one piece of candied fruit. The orange juice she served in a tiny glass, hardly larger than a shot glass. I don't know how poor we were, though I suspect not as poor as the poverty that they feared would return someday. We lived, in the 1960s, as though in the shadow of the Great Depression and World War II before the war's outcome was known. Regardless of how much time we put between ourselves and the past, the Great Depression haunted every room of the household even as late as the 1970s. You could hear the past at night, scratching like squirrels building their cache in the attic. The bare, spindly shadow of the miser wavered on the wall of my room at night. Whenever I pulled open what one usually thinks of as the kitchen junk drawer, there in the corner, beside the containers full of saved rubber bands, used twist ties, corks, and brittle canning gaskets, was an old Velveeta box filled with ration coupons and blue or red round cardboard tokens the size of a penny or a dime. Vestiges of the New Deal. They must have been saving these, imagining a future in which these few saved items gave us an advantage that I in my pitiful ignorance couldn't yet understand.

❧

It has cleared off this afternoon and turned cold. There is a little snow on the tops of the ridges from this morning's storm. Lining the city streets of the past and the present, the maples are still holding on to a few bright leaves. And in my kitchen now, as in the past, there burns the alchemist's fire. A scummy beige sponge rises in my grandmother's bread bowl, and soon the oven will warm with the aroma of loaves browning in her folded tin bread pans. The soup she made for me simmers in her cast-iron Dutch oven, alongside the enamel vat full of mealy Gravensteins bubbling into sauce. I hold her masher in my fist, the hickory handle worn smooth by generations of arthritic claws that mine resemble a little more with each passing year. I crush the mushy yellow flesh from the orchard, pour in sugar, dust it with cinnamon, reach inside the oven to tap crusts, stir the soup, sip from her spoon, and add such savory and pepper as would have intoxicated her, in whose face the blush turned grey as the sink water she saved and re-used for days.

She cried, "No! Please! No!" when, near the end of her life, I finally jerked the chain and unstopped the drain for the last time.

When I handed her little wizened body across the threshold into the arms of the routine medics, who then hauled her away, the air filled with the hysterical fear of scarcity and loneliness that she carried like a hunchback all her life. Such is the coagulum of despair that breathes in a kitchen. *Solve et coagula,* dissolve and coagulate, so the alchemists called this transformation, this rain of purified matter that is gratitude for what does and does not sustain us.

AUGURIES OF ABSENCE

Our local wild predators—wolves, mountain lions, and bears—are our neighbors here in northeastern Oregon. We don't so much encounter them as we observe their absence in the fresh signs of their recent proximity—tracks pressed into snow, mud, or dust—winter, spring, summer, and fall. Accompanying these near encounters is our uncanny sense of being seen by others invisible to us. One day we find the place in the snow where a mountain lion sat to survey the canyon below him, his forepaws and haunches pressed into the fresh snow and his long tail making a fan behind him before he leaped down the slope as we approached. Here are the ovals a pack of wolves left where they slept, then woke as one and slipped off into the forest as we entered the meadow at dawn. On the occasions when we do see them, they typically "flee from me that sometime did me seek." In that moment when our eyes fix on the eyes of a mother and her yearling mountain lion, I'm certain that Thomas Wyatt had something else in mind than either the lions or my constant companion and I have in ours.

As we walked down the trail from the Minam Rim last Sunday morning, we experienced the usual absences of bears. We intended to visit the daughter of friends, the daughter being also a dear friend of our sons with whom we miss sharing these rambles. She is camping this summer along the Little Minam River, performing a salmon and bull trout survey with a crew of Oregon Department of Fish and Wildlife seasonal employees. As we descended, each of the three groups of horse packers who passed us, returning from their weekend camping trips in the canyon below, asked if we were armed, warning that other campers in the canyon had bears in camp each night. It so happened we weren't armed, though I thought earlier in the day to bring bear spray and bells to attach to our packs. It so happened that I left both the bells and the pepper spray on the counter in the kitchen.

The Minam Canyon is renowned for bears—black bears though, not grizzlies, which were extirpated nearly a century ago, occasional unconfirmed sightings in the Wallowas notwithstanding. It's true that black bears are completely capable of similar acts of mayhem as grizzlies, though walking in the presence of the latter tends to sharpen one's attention more than the former. In the case of my attentive walking in grizzly bear habitat, substitutes for *attentive* might include long periods of insouciant walking punctuated by brief episodes of walking in paranoid fear. When we reached her camp, our friend's daughter—and other members of the ODFW fish crew—confirmed that a black bear turned over their food boxes one night and smashed one on another.

No sooner did we reach the bottom of the canyon, twenty-five hundred feet below the rim, than we started seeing big rotted logs turned over by bears searching for galleries of honeydew and their attendant ants. Seeing this, there was suddenly a song I felt I needed to sing very loudly. Afterwards, Josefa and I chattered manically, trying to make as much noise as possible so as not to startle a temperamental ursine who may be in a family way.

Despite bear sign, we saw no bears, and after a dip in the river and lunch with our young friend, we began the slow ascent back to the rim. Ascending, unlike descending, tends to turn one's thoughts inward, as the combination of steepness, sun, heat, and dust—and the physical discomfort they cause—are a little distracting; ascending, that is, causes some physical discomfort such as those regal others on mount earlier in the day are very pleased to avoid. Soon, I was thinking about the first time I was ever in the presence of a bear. The presence, even the invisible presence, of bears tends to cause Josefa and I to make lists of these encounters and outcomes. Two years ago, when we saw not one but five grizzlies in one summer, she started compiling a lifelong list of bears seen, both from a car and, more exhilarating for sure, in the wild. It was a good long list. I think there were eighteen bears on it, though I'm sure it remained incomplete.

Climbing out of Minam Canyon, I remembered that my first encounter with a bear, which we neglected to include on that list two years ago, was in Virginia's Blue Ridge Mountains, where my mother's parents took me for the first time on their August holiday in 1966. We drove into Big Meadows campground late in the day, and the first thing we heard upon arrival was to keep our food in the car because a bear was raiding the camp.

A bear? This was exciting news to me, though I'm not sure I had any idea exactly what a bear was or might be, or that bears existed in any world I lived in. The three bears with their porridge and beds were the only bears I knew of. That a bear could perturb the ordinary state of affairs, well, that was something maybe to admire. Something to think about at least. There was a kind of pleasurable tension in that campground, everybody a little more animated than usual, talkative, neighborly, full of stories of sights and signs, and all because of a bear. Life in a National Park campground seemed a little better than back home in Ohio. Plus, I'm 83.7 percent certain that nobody in that campground was armed.

We never saw that Blue Ridge bear either, but the holiday was no less exceptional because of it. The next morning, there was frost on the ground. The air was crisp, and we felt more alive, breakfast tasted better, and my grandparents seemed more affectionate toward each other.

Our last night in the Appalachians we camped near Mount Mitchell, "the highest point in the Eastern United States," my grandfather said with great solemnity. The next morning, we would drive northwestward and through the Cumberland Gap on our way back to Ohio. We pitched our tent under blossoming rhododendrons. Not one of us remarked about the dense shrubs arched over our Baker tent with the "gypsy striped" awnings we hung from the dining fly at night for privacy.

At dusk, we walked to a meadow that overlooked a gap between hills and stood there looking west in silence. The youngest didn't know exactly what the others were thinking or what they saw. What I saw were vast planes of color: the zenith dark blue, fading to paler blue, to a thin horizon of roiling scarlet, valleys between hills filled with violet fog, the night rising from pores deep in earth to meet its descent from the sky. And this I knew was Beauty, a consolation for the mining wastes we left behind back home in Ohio. Beauty, I understood, is something therefore journeyed toward, an exception to the mundane ugliness of American life, an entirely parallel universe from which mailbags full of garish postcards are shipped daily, first class. That scenery failed to convince me, young as I was, only because the evening's transparency was a pretext, a pose that disguises the disfigured places we'd left behind, to say nothing of how those places affected the quality of our lives, to which we were about to return. In this, I surely recognized the melancholy of late Sunday afternoons as we returned to Alliance from the family farm whenever we "went visiting."

That night, though, we decided to sleep outside the tent, under the stars, or rather, under the rhododendrons, and without a thought about bears. The air beneath those shrubs seemed redolent at dawn, sun filtering through gaudy pink petals: first light, an almost-dream of the womb I only exited eight years before.

No bears ever again announced their presence in my childhood or its environs. Still, that week in the Appalachians when I first became aware of bears continued to haunt me as I rambled in the forests, marshes, and farm fields near Alliance. When I left home for college, I encountered for the first time a particular strain of American Romanticism when I read Faulkner's famous short story, "The Bear," and the exaltation of the wilderness in his prose. But what struck me most vividly then and that haunts me still is something my teacher said as we discussed the killing of Old Ben. "That was a clear transgression," he told us sophomores, "and pretty much explains everything that has gone wrong since our founding. If it's not the original sin of America, there are after all so many, it stands as a plausible sign for each—the genocide of its First People and the enslavement of Africans."

I would have to move to the rural American West before wild predators became a lived—that is, everyday—reality, though when I briefly returned to Ohio for graduate school in Athens in the mid-1980s, we lived far out in the countryside south of town, where, one autumn, a bear did pass through the hollows nearby, rooting through garbage habitually thrown into the eroded gully in our neighbor's overgrazed pasture, causing their hounds to suffer conniptions of bloodlust. I was given at that time to delusional interpretations of natural phenomena as prophetic signs of metaphysical intention suggestive, in this case, of the apocalyptic collapse of capitalism and the return of Faulkner's primordial wilderness. Romanticism, that is, had had its way with me.

Later still, while living in Germany, I felt a more tempered sense of visionary hope in the future when a bear thought to have across the Alps from Italy appeared in Bayern, the first recorded sighting of any bear in Germany in one hundred eighty years, so the media reported at the time. Farmers were outraged when the bear raided bee hives, and though the bear survived long enough to attract defenders in the public, the farmers, who definitely *were* armed, soon shot and killed that errant bear.

Any evidence of re-wilding is, I suspect, a cause of much human anxiety and subsequent brutality toward what only wants to go on living. "Are you armed?" the horse packers asked, meaning that the presence of bears is a challenge to human prerogative. In each of those subsequent cases, in Ohio and Bayern, and the threat we didn't take seriously enough in the opinion of the horse packers, it was the presence of bears in their ecological household that not only alerted me but delighted and gave me a hopeful sense of the possible. And what else is possible if not a sense of solidarity with our neighbors, these non-human people with whom we could make peace if we both could be present and unmolested by mortal fear of the other?

FROM A SLOW TRAIN

We'd booked the express to Zurich, but when a double-decker backed into the station at the platform, something seemed wrong. A closer inspection of our tickets and departures board confirmed, though day and platform were correct, our train was an IC, an InterCity, not an ICE, an InterCity *Express,* that aerodynamic miracle designed to speed passengers to their destinations at a smooth two hundred kilometers per hour. No wonder the tickets weren't expensive! It was going to be a long day chugging south through the upper Rhine Valley, which isn't such a terrible thing after all.

Given the likelihood of things going wrong, a slow train is often no slower than an express. A week earlier, we'd booked seats on the ICE to Freiburg, but a strong thunderstorm slowed the trains that day and we missed—by an hour—our connection in Karlsruhe. There were twice as many passengers as seats by then, so instead of reserved seating, we found ourselves standing on the next express among a group of trekkers headed to the Schwarzwald, crowded in next to an overburdened WC.

Several days later, on our return trip from Freiburg, a man nearby on the platform noticed our puzzlement. We wondered if, according to the posted seating chart, we were standing in the proper place to best access our coach? If, in a rush, you've ever jumped onto a crowded train far from your assigned coach, then pushed through every coach to find your seat, you know that boarding properly avoids making a spectacle and nuisance of yourself in aisles crowded by young mothers folding strollers, trekkers wrestling rucksacks, and retirees burdened by enormous luggage. The man who approached us was eager to practice his English and assured us we were in precisely the right place. We chatted a while, then his train arrived. Not a moment later, even as he waved, the dreaded word *Verspätung* appeared on the crawler.

Our train had been delayed. If you have a connection to make, a voice from above announced, please visit the information desk: you are going to miss it. At the information desk, our hunchbacked German and the Deutschebahn employee's similarly gestural English kept coming around to the word *Selbst-mord*. The word's meaning is obvious—it's a compound after all, both parts are cognates. The DB employee started to mime the situation, with a silly grin on her face, when suddenly our linguistic gears meshed. "*Ach so! Enschuldigung!*" We lowered our heads, ashamed. This was embarrassing. Our inconvenience, indeed! The delay had been caused by no act of god. Some sad bastard had leaped in front of the train twenty kilometers south of the station. Our train, plausibly on time only moments before, would be delayed by "approximately sixty minutes" as authorities euphemistically "cleared the track of an obstruction."

It's uncharitable, actually it's *shitty,* to think such thoughts, but exasperation seemed inevitable: that poor fellow who stepped in front of the express threw everything and everyone *off schedule.* Many a rendezvous was thwarted. Connections missed. Delays cascading down the line, hundreds, perhaps thousands of us agitated. Around us, those who had someone to call, called and uttered the inevitable, "*ach!*" Such, we might suppose, is the satisfaction of self-slaughter's claim on our attention. And maybe,

the death of the despairing fellow notwithstanding, all this interruption of the orderly function of the ordinary world isn't such a
bad thing. In a way, and totally irrespective of the actual circumstances, *the guy made a plausibly good point.*

Boarding that fast, comfortable train in Freiburg, even knowing we'd no chance of making our original connection in Karlsruhe, everyone found a seat with a welcome but weary sigh. Poor
bastard. Too bad for his family. We were soon underway, and that
saddest man in the world that day returned to the small confines
of local fame. The machinery was running again and making up
for lost time. It so happened that the train was only thirty minutes late and were soon in Karlsruhe, and though we missed the
express to Stuttgart, instead we made our way onto a crowded late
afternoon inter-city crammed with commuters and one screaming child.

On the slow train to Switzerland a week later, it was much the
same as that commuter train from Karlsruhe, every ten or twenty minutes letting off a loud and cheerful group of retirees on an
outing to the birthplace of a local seventeenth-century celebrity
renowned for clock making, wood carving, astronomical discovery, or lens grinding. The train likewise opened, gathering in or
discharging commuters who work at the rural tool and die factory. Teachers herded their charges and baggage for an end-of-year
outing to a not-entirely-exotic town across a border of one kind
or another, where they visited an interesting church, a museum of
early steam-powered engines, or a local tradition of ornate lock-
smithing. That day we changed trains four times. We also changed
platforms three, with no more than two minutes between trains
during to descend into the fearsome tunnels below tracks, then
ascend hopefully to the proper platform. Each train promised to
be slower and smaller than the previous one.

Just before our last transfer, everyone beginning to reach above
their seats to pull down bags or adjust rucksacks, an unlucky rail

worker stumbled backwards into the oncoming train ahead of us. Our train slowed to a stop five kilometers shy of Interlaken. Perched above the blue waters of the Thunersee, enormous Alps on either side of us, we watched sailboats lean hard with the wind, fair-weather cumulus passing under the peak of the Faulhorn. The conductor spoke to local riders in an incomprehensible dialect and they casually exited the train. This caused everyone else to experience an increasing sense of dread. When someone tried to exit, the conductor, now speaking reasonable German, explicitly prevented our doing so. A Chinese student asked if I thought it possible to walk the rest of the way. I advised against it. An hour passed. The train sat emptied out of its Swiss passengers, while our little United Nations of puzzlement wondered what was going on. Soon the conductor who forbade us from exiting the train disappeared. Without a word then, when a bus arrived outside the nearby station, those who remained on board grabbed rucksacks and rushed the exits. When we emerged from the tunnel below the tracks there sat all the Swiss passengers, waiting to get on the same bus.

The next station, it turned out, wasn't where we would meet the next train; we needed to transfer on yet another bus. By the time we arrived at Interlaken Ost, our train was pulling away from the platform. A setback for sure but only temporary, as trains depart for Grindelwald every thirty minutes. We'd time on our hands to discover that Goethe, the Prince of Poets, was partly responsible for our situation, being as he was an early advocate of the area as a destination. His poem *"Gesang der Geister über den Wassern"* was posted on a signboard. Song of the spirit over the waters. Yes, and why not? Blame it on the poets!

The next train departed with us onboard. And so, nine, instead of seven, hours after leaving Stuttgart, our electric cog train clunked to a halt, the driver turned off the power, and the car suddenly went still. We gathered our rucksacks and stepped down from the train into the glories of the Bernese Oberland summer.

～o～

As a boy, I was prone to wearing costumes, and I recall a time when I dressed as a train engineer. A train engineer's uniform amounted to a striped billed cap cut from pillow ticking, a red bandana, chambray shirt, square-cut denim jacket with blanket lining, and "engineer boots." That was the costume of a children's TV show host, Captain Penny. I even owned a signed black and white glossy photo of the captain tipping his hat. Today, the boots of this reverie would be less associated with railroaders than motorcycle enthusiasts of the more obnoxious sort—late middle-aged, white men in leather jackets embroidered with "Toledo Hog Fuckers," said hogs parked outside Carl Jr.'s. Said motorcyclists are better funded than was I as a child. My grandfather, who denied me nothing, accumulated small amounts of change into "The Davy Fund." It was from this account he drew to purchase my only pair of engineer boots. This permitted me to parade my fantasy around the house, "Whoo-Whoo, all aboard!" until after a couple months my feet outgrew the boots.

It's difficult to pinpoint the moment when trains so impressed me that I wanted to drive one or wear the proper uniform to do so. The desire felt innate. My grandfather cherished his Lionel Train set that came out during holidays—a Baltimore and Ohio Streamliner engine and freight cars. Lurid tales of accidents at unguarded crossings also were common fare, calculated to terrify me into never leaving the house. The death of the blonde bombshell, Jayne Mansfield, the working man's Marilyn Monroe, was portrayed as a train accident at a crossing that resulted in her being decapitated, which wasn't exactly true (she'd been in an accident with a tractor trailer) though the didactic intention of the lie—*exercise extreme caution at train crossings!*—asserts itself in my mind every time I cross the tracks.

Regardless, trains became a permanent fascination. There were abandoned trolley tracks in the undeveloped fields behind the tract house my parents built on Pleasant Place. Those steel rails vanished into what my mother referred to as "poverty grass," a term so vague it covers any number of species, though she meant *Danthonia spicata*. It's possible I remember seeing these tracks, which led southwest of town toward Louisville, Ohio. What I've come to think of as *my* memory, though, is from a world that existed prior to the one into which I was born. That prior world was rapidly vanishing under the post–World War II construction boom. The trollies were gone; nevertheless, my grandfather's memory so thoroughly occupied my imagination I hardly distinguished his memory from mine. As a young man during the Great Depression he took that trolley all the way to Minerva, where he played semi-professional football for the legendary Merchants while courting my grandmother, a farm girl from nearby New Kensington. I remember this all very clearly. It was in 1933, a quarter century before my birth, when the trolley rattled alongside the old mosquito-infested Ohio Canal. Trains conveyed us then toward sport and love.

Soon after 1933 trains would be conveying people, many of them my kinsmen, not only toward love, but toward their murders. Even as a child in the early 1960s, I knew this history as I lay in bed, listening as trains passed south of Pleasant Place on the other side of the woods and marshes that separated town from countryside.

That line was soon abandoned; the trains of my youth mostly passed just outside my family's store on the north side of town, where steel and manufacturing plants operated, surrounded by the black ghetto that remains to this day, depopulated as factories closed and jobs disappeared. The rail yard lay just across Patterson Avenue and behind the grain mill. Main lines converged from all four directions. A rickety one-lane viaduct spanned the tracks and connected Patterson Avenue with downtown. Our store lay along the northern line and whenever a shunting engine or a fast train came through, the storefront shook on its foundations.

Throughout the day, the crossing closed as shunting engines moved manufactured goods from one factory or another to build the trains that sent those goods to market. The smaller engines puttered for hours, so that our customers had to reroute around the railyard through downtown and over the viaduct or the little-used underpass several blocks north on Webb Avenue. There wasn't much reason for customers to go to this trouble of finding a route to Axelrod Auto Parts, however, as there were automotive stores accessible on the other side of the tracks. The closed crossing gates and narrow bridge even cut us off from half of the black ghetto that lived south of the tracks. If location is the shibboleth of realtors, then ours was the limiting factor to actually doing business at all. I hardly cared, as engineers waving from the engines and the railcars full of manufactured goods following them brought endlessly fascinating news from elsewhere, and an early source of longing to run away.

In the summer of 1963, my mother and I often ran away from Alliance, though usually only for a night or two. Several times we visited friends of hers, the Coopers, who lived in Maximo. A crossroads west of town, Maximo amounted to a a small corner grocery and a blinking red light at an intersection. The husband of this couple, Bill, had survived the airplane accident that my father hadn't. Their Victorian farmhouse sat beside what must have been the east-west main line that passed not far from our family store. The trains along that line seldom slowed as they passed west through town, and by the time they made the big curve outside of Maximo, the locomotives seemed to be traveling at escape velocity. After the locomotive roared past, I cried out, "It must be going like sixty!"—a speed approximating the upward limits of natural law.

As night came on, the hills and air around me and the Coopers's children turned violet. The grass in the orchard began to feel cold to our bare feet, and we heard the distant Streamliner approach. We gaze down the track as far as we could see. One of us put an ear to the track. We glowed with anxiety and exhilaration as we awaited the locomotive. The anticipation made us giddy about what we couldn't yet see, and because when it did appear, like a towering black wave, it was upon us in an instant. An inconceivably powerful machine, a diesel tsunami. Aerodynamic precursor of the bullet train, the apogee of Modernist design. The roar of the Streamliner peaked, then quickly diminished as the boxcars clattered by. And when the caboose passed, a hand waved and a lantern swung in the dark.

"And what is a caboose?" the innocent might ask today.

❧

Probably one of the first songs you sang along to was "I've Been Workin' on the Railroad," whose lyrics seem suggestive of matters beyond the usual scope of childish experience. Wise to this already, older siblings dared us innocents to replace one crucial pronoun in the chorus so that the song would refer, not to a safety device, but to fellatio, whatever that was. We younger children pretended that we didn't require any explanation of the snickering metaphor. Introduced in Mrs. Morgan's kindergarten, by the end of first grade our class could stand on stage before our mothers and their glistening eyes to sing it as an unmistakably profane, three-part round.

There were many songs we learned, however, that spoke of a deep melancholy associated with trains. The chorus of "Five Hundred Miles," with its train whistle that can be heard dopplering over the horizon, still chokes me with sorrow, though so far as I'm aware no one I loved ever missed the train I was on. My grandfather sang Elizabeth Cotton's cheerfully up-tempo (though it expressed a degree of regret over having to exit life, a sorrow only a train might salve) "Freight Train." The complex content of the verses of "John Henry" never registered in my childhood mind. Whatever "The Wabash Cannonball" celebrated completely escaped me, though its celebratory list of American place names and joyous expression of the urge to keep moving was a cultural imperative that brings me to my feet, eager to dance or sing along, whether I encounter that list, for example, in Bobby Troupe's joyous highway song, "Route 66," or Stephen Vincent Benet's "American Names," with its melancholy ultimate line referencing Wounded Knee.

But always in my memory those two categories of train rides in songs: trains of failure and loss; trains of hope and redemption. Later, I would sing along to "Hear My Train a-Comin'," "Love in Vain," "People Get Ready," "One After 909," and "Casey Jones." And later still, "She Caught the Katy," "Choo Choo Ch'Boogie," "Broke Down Engine," "Mystery Train," "This Train," "The Train I Ride," "Freedom Train," and "Glory Train." And there will always be that train a no-good woman rides. And much later still, Little Richard's and Fishbone's unhinged cover of Leadbelly's "Rock Island Line." But there were subcategories of railroad songs, such as dismemberment songs like Maggie Bell's and Long John Baldry's plaintive "In the Pines," another Leadbelly classic, in which the head of the plaintive singer's father was found, but his body never was. My hands-down favorite decapitation train song is Dave Van Ronk's version of Lawrence Block's "Georgie and the IRT," whose crucial verses describe the hapless commuter, Georgie, getting himself cut in half by the train door. In mock heroic verses the decapitated head of our hero is carried to Flatbush, his vulgar last words resounding.

But one train song transcends all categories, expressing both the melancholy of aspirations crushed and the sacred allegiances of love. That train ride was on the Soul Train line, and it was "The Midnight Train to Georgia," by Gladys Knight and the Pips. In high school my friends and I sang and danced along. With Harriet, Laurel, and Linda, as Pips and me (an incongruous fourth), doing our very best syncopated steps, we responded soulfully, "whoo whoo," to Gladys', aka our friend Bill's, cry that he'd rather live with his many in whatever world they find than live without him, alone.

~&~

The truth about passenger trains is that they had succumbed entirely by the 1970s to the hegemony of cursed automobiles. The passenger train that ran during my earlier childhood was shabby, a debauched divorcée at the end of the bar picking at the cherry in a watery Manhattan, shaking her bottle-blonde head in disbelief that it all came down to *this*. Decades before taggers and hyperbolic graffiti, paint on the freight trains that filled the windows of our family's storefront in no way helped brighten prospects for train travel. Engines, passenger and freight cars gave the impression of having been parked for two hundred years outside a coal-burning power plant. Theirs was the color palette of the woebegone.

Our local passenger trains were relics of the Great Depression, their exteriors faded brown, interiors gray, seats soiled, cracked, and frayed. After World War II, perhaps it was inevitable that Americans abandoned trains for automobiles. People simply had ridden inside enough of these derelict passenger cars, and now preferred the privacy and freedom to roam wherever they chose in a Hudson. No more bleak rail stations. Instead: gas stations and Howard Johnson's!

In kindergarten, the PTA took us on our first, not to be mistaken for first-class, outing: a short train trip to Canton, Ohio, after which we bused back to Alliance. For many decades, it remained my only train trip. It was 1963, and my mother's mother accompanied me. Someone called the passage under the tracks to the platform the "Alliance subway." This failed to provoke irony as intended; rather I thought of a dimly lit, dangerous place where old men in shabby jackets and stained trousers offer children boxes of Chicklets. How much of this anxiety was communicated by the disgust on their faces I can't say, but the mothers' glow of prissiness in heels, pencil skirts, and pillbox hats illuminated the underground and led us to safety.

Did we wait for our train to Canton among the jaded glories of an old station the wealth of our local nineteenth-century steel barons built? No. Nothing of the sort.

There is, however, a rare postcard photograph of Alliance's first train station, which was built in 1853. An octagonal two-story wood frame building, with one-story east and west wings, it burned down ten years later, but not before it was the scene of a visit by Abraham Lincoln on his way to Washington, DC, for his first inauguration. The president-elect spoke briefly, but with characteristically comic understatement: "I appear before you merely to greet you and say farewell. I have no time for long speeches. . . . If I should make a speech at every town, I would not get to Washington until sometime after the inauguration. But as I am somewhat interested in the inauguration, I would like to get there." His words, the newspaper reported, were greeted with chuckles.

The original station was replaced by a brick station that occupied the same triangle of land formed by the intersection of the north-south and east-west rail lines, the acute X one observed from the viaduct above. That station was torn down by 1952, but the platforms, with their ornate Victorian iron-work roof supports topped by tarnished copper roofing, remained, as did the subterranean passage connecting the two. In the pastel-colored postcard of the second station, the platforms are crowded with passengers heading west, while a man in a suit and bowler hat stands between the rails of the northbound train, hands in his pockets, looking for the telltale smoke of the approaching steam engine. That station's demise six years before my birth robbed us of grandeur, as it was replaced by a one-story brick building that had the institutional appeal of a welfare office or suburban police station. After decades of cheerless decline and soul-deadening bleakness, that mid-twentieth-century station was replaced by a small, *yuckish-mickafivish* brick and natural stone station with faux Victorian replica lampposts that, modest as it all is, seems an improvement. Two passenger trains pause each day at those platforms in my broken-hearted, post-industrial hometown.

❧

When I moved west after graduating from university, I lived in a series of small mill towns, where there happened to be a good deal of rail traffic, moving mostly lumber from local mills and coal from mines in Utah, Wyoming, and eastern Montana. Waking early on a summer morning in a neighborhood on the north side of Missoula, the air would smell sweet with the scent of freshly cut ponderosa and Douglas fir piled high on the log decks at the mill near our former company house. During the Reagan years, timber cutting on the National Forests throughout the Pacific Northwest was prodigious, resulting in an overcut that soon shut down the logging industry. That first full summer in Montana, the smell of pitch on a cool morning filled me with the satisfactions of the exotic. Here was a form of industrial work that seemed far removed from the boarded-over factories of my Rust Belt hometown. The industrial base of Missoula would disappear once all the available trees on public lands were cut and shipped overseas. Missoula, like many western cities, would lose its working-class character, substituting it with an upper-middle-class consumer mendacity that a generation of younger people today must assume is just an old cultural norm.

In Montana at that time there were rail lines new to me, principally the Burlington Northern with its engines painted pine-forest green. And because the air was so often cool, still, and clear, the humidity hovering fifty percentage points or more below what I was accustomed to, one could hear the trains as they powered westward through the Hellgate Canyon into the broad Missoula Valley—but that was a distant and plaintive cry. To this day, living in eastern Oregon where the atmospheric conditions are similar, I can hear the far-off sound of the Union Pacific locomotives entering or exiting the Grand Ronde Valley; when it's dry, the locomotives sound like distraught cattle bellowing at the windowsill.

The most astonishing sound related to railroads, though, is one first heard while we lived on the north side of Missoula not far from the railyard, on Defoe Street, one of dozens of similar streets named after British writers—Byron, Burns, Cowper, Burton, among others, with a Hawthorne and a Cooper thrown in to represent American writers so as not to seem to privilege one of our two great nations over the other, though we remain divided, as the saying goes, by a common language. Winters in the Northern Rockies can be desperately cold, though on the west side of the Continental Divide winters were more moderate, affected by the Pacific as much as cold continental high pressure from central Canada and northern Great Plains. On occasion, though, cold air slips west through mountain passes and brings arctic air into an area that stretches from Spokane to Boise to Missoula and all points between. One late winter night on Defoe Street we heard something like a dissonant chorus of oddly pitched bells ringing. It was metallic sounding, and weirdly angelic. I put down my book and went to the door. Never having heard anything quite like it before, I went outside in my pacs, mittens, and parka. Beneath the ringing, there was the familiar sound of railcars being shunted around the yard, the switchmen coupling railcars, building freight trains. That bizarre tintinnabulation was the sound of cold wheels moving along cold rails and braking as the coupling neared.

When we arrived in eastern Oregon in 1988, the rail yard in La Grande still had an active brick roundhouse and many parallel tracks in the shunting yard full of freight trains. Best of all, Amtrak and its Pioneer passenger train still pulled up to the platform outside the station, where we waited for relatives coming to visit us on trains that were reliable only in the sense that they were always late. Our sons, accompanied by their mother, also enjoyed a memorable train ride with our oldest son's kindergarten class on the Pioneer to Pendleton, forty-five miles west over the Blue Mountains. That passenger train passed through Meacham Canyon, forested in the bottom but surrounded by high, grassy hogbacks where herds of elk still graze, stalked now by packs of wolves or solitary mountain lions, and where one can also sometimes spot a wandering black bear.

Not long after we arrived in La Grande, Union Pacific centralized its eastern Oregon operations farther west near Hermiston; passing along the highway at night, one can see the lights of the massive rail yard. Sadly, our local roundhouse and its rotating circle of tracks is gone, torn down and bricks hauled away. The Pioneer ceased long ago to run between Denver and Portland. The rail yard that once seemed alive with men and trains looks desolate. Most days it's empty.

There is a local excursion train whose engines sometimes show up in La Grande, but its terminal is north of here in a nearby town. This county-owned railroad, much criticized by disgruntled anti-government types, connects La Grande and the remote town of Enterprise. That spur once moved agricultural and forest products, but recently served as a parking lot for old railcars no longer in use. The county paid off the cost of the rail line purchase by renting out the rails for decommissioned rail cars. A bit unsightly. That *was* a complaint, but not the one our anti-government cranks made about the abomination of public ownership. For them, the truest expression of American Constitutional guarantees is freedom from the hell of others. These critics, however, are assuaged when the train actually runs because it's "robbed" at gunpoint by masked actors on horseback who block the tracks and enter the coaches armed.

⌁

Our lack of public transport raises the problem of social isolation, which is only made worse by automobiles. So much that we take for granted militates against having any connection with others. Automobiles and freeways (an ironic misnomer at virtually all times of the day and night) are perfect symbols of our atomization, reinforcing isolation, loneliness, and contempt for others. As Peter Sloterdijk puts it, "Have we not become the isolated thing-for-yourself in the middle of similar beings?" In an automobile, we're most certainly not in this together. Everyone is simply annoying, and getting in our way, and their political beliefs, reduced to a few words on that repulsive bumper sticker, likely infuriate us. This level of contempt is difficult to sustain on a train.

Josefa and I once glided westward toward Paris Est as a group of German women, ranging from late youth to middle age, made a spectacle of themselves chattering and laughing loudly in an atypically German manner for nine o'clock in the morning. Why were they not quietly and grimly assessing their souls? Come on ladies, quiet down. Well, they didn't, and listening to them joke with each other about the outrageous fun that awaited them in Paris, how much good wine they planned to drink, and how handsome French men are, I felt happy about their prospects. There are few instances I can think of where a passing automobile and its passenger's happiness was ever so accessible, or much less became my own.

If one is on anything besides a commuter train or subway, someone is bound to strike up a conversation. True, some people, ourselves included, are shy about striking up conversations with strangers. Sometimes events are such that fellow passengers must share an ironic pleasantry about, for example, the armed guards who just passed through the coach or the publicly drunk teenager who poured a Radler all over the floor and whom the entire coach openly criticizes for his lack of respect for others. At other times, you keep catching someone's eye, until, close to the destination, a question finally gets asked and a curiosity satisfied in desperately truncated conversation.

On a train trip from München to Stuttgart, returning late Sunday from a weekend of glorious skiing in Obersdorf, we'd reserved seats at a table, meaning two other passengers would be seated across from us as we travelled from Bayern to the capital of Baden-Württemberg. As we left the station, three of us studiously bent over our notebooks or novels, but the fourth interrupted, peeved at us for our antisocial behavior. "What good students we are!" We three looked up and laughed because his subtext was correct: we were being rude. Our interlocutor, we learned, was a businessman who worked in Stuttgart but lived in München, where he spent his weekends with family. And, small world of wonders, our other companion, a student at the Kunstakademie, knew a former student of ours in the United States. We made small talk about our novels, coursework, and various pleasures until (it seemed so soon) we pulled into Stuttgart main station.

Here in La Grande, once in a great while, the melancholy atmosphere surrounding the absence of passenger trains evaporates and genuine excitement rolls into the local rail yard, bringing us together despite our cable news preferences. Besides the annual mock robbery of the excursion train, there is on occasion a vintage engine that arrives, billowing smoke and steam, like the 1915 Baldwin engine called the Blue Goose that recently returned after a sixty-five-year-long absence. Such arrivals are announced in the newspaper well in advance, and I've found myself more than a few times standing on the viaduct with a dozen mostly eccentric parents or grandparents, youngsters in tow, waiting for the tell-tale column of smoke in the distance, and then the unmistakable throaty sound of the steam whistle at crossings. Some years, Santa arrives by train. Mostly, though, trains appear regularly only in the obituaries, where we learn that Orville or Harold or Bill start-ed working for the railroad in 1948, 1952, or 1960. Here in east-ern Oregon, anyway, railroads are not so much an opportunity to establish social cohesion as they are, in the words of my teacher long ago, "the end of a lot of ending."

❧

In the late 1990s, when we began to travel abroad on busman's holidays, arranging part-time teaching to fund our travel, my con-stant companion and I began to rediscover the pleasures of riding trains. In exchange for six weeks or six months of lecturing, we could live, as our parents' and especially grandparents' generation did, with public transport delivering us to distant cities, neighbor-hoods, and alpine trailheads. It's odd to recall that earlier genera-tions of Americans were familiar with these before the automobile and its oil-drenched grip on our lives.

What a relief to be spared having to drive a car in a foreign city—or any city, really—but rather to arrive at the main station in Amsterdam and buy tickets for the tram that delivered us to our hotel and then, soon after, several blocks from our friend's flat. *This* is pleasure. Or to ride the ICE that delivered us to Ulm, where we'd just enough time to walk out of the station and into the square to stand in awe of the cathedral, the mountain of heav-en towering above us, before boarding the regional express to

Obersdorf to ski in the Alps for the first time, virtually every seat occupied by someone bearing Nordic or downhill skis.

Or even the dubious privilege of riding the London Tube, which surprises with its lovely randomness. So long as the electric isn't cut, and the cars don't go dark, one is definitely privileged to hear (and bathe in) the languages of the former empire on which the sun didn't set. Or to be on a train to the airport early one morning, it must be dawn of New Year's Day, reviving a passenger who enjoyed herself a little too much the night before. I held her in my arms, trying to keep her awake as others rushed for help. In every case, with the possible exception of the ICE whose tickets are expensive, one is thrust into the world with its infinite variety of people, most of whom haven't so much an interest in meeting you as they do in covertly and slyly observing you, inventing the narrative of your life. Isn't that public life as public transport makes it possible? Always caught between private confidence and public shyness?

One can look out the window at passing scenery, though on a fast train this can become a bit nauseating. There is an alp out there, a lake, or a village that appears as though from the mist and forests in a nineteenth-century painting by Karl David Friedrich. Or one can read a novel, the newspaper, or perhaps, god help you, the Deutsche Bahn magazine. Besides a few teenagers, most people are not wearing earbuds, and if they are sitting with someone they know, they may share the sandwich bought at the station this morning, chat away, or people-watch as they pour a wholesome thermos of warm cocoa into each other's cups.

Looking over his shoulder, I see one day that a guy with dreads is reading *The Epic of Gilgamesh*. When he senses I'm reading over his shoulder, he turns to me and I flush. Sorry, mate. On the platform, a young woman is engrossed in . . . good grief, a novel by Robert Musil. And on the way to Freiburg, a father seated with his children is reading . . . hmm, must be *The Radetzky March*.

There are also less bookish types furtively reading *Fifty Shades of Gray*, surreptitiously masturbating both in the original language or in translation. I can't, however, choose the library of the train passengers any more than I can choose who gets on or off the train. I assume there must be an algorithm for this sort of thing. In the seats across from us, one young man is reading a book titled *Quantifying Uncertainty*.

On a train from Colmar to Stuttgart, we found our second-class compartment in the very front of the train, a tiny quarter-coach with room enough for no more than a dozen passengers. The WC was right outside the glass divider, so we had an unfortunate perspective. As we crossed the border, two armed police officers entered the car to look us over, the female officer behind the first to enter, a hand on her revolver. This was unnerving. In complete silence, the first officer looked into everyone's face and eventually failed to see what he was looking for there. Soon, not soon enough really, they left the car. Later, a young Muslim woman, fully covered in a blue burqa, and accompanied by her several children, came forward from first class to use the WC. Her children, her young son especially, wasn't pleased with being left to his own devices while she peed. The other children followed and soon surrounded the door, pounding on it. When the door flew open, a very young mother stood there, uncovered, in plaid green shorts and a pink T-shirt, looking pretty much like any other twenty-year-old. She covered herself, and as I recalled similar situations from classical literature that didn't turn out well for the observer, I looked away as she exited to her concealed world.

⌀

Last week, as we made our way south along the Rhine toward Zurich on that slow train, we passed through Rottweil in southwest Germany. On the far platform near the station stood a young father and his adolescent sons. The older, perhaps ten years old,

wore glasses and a ball cap and stood pensively with his hands behind his back. They stood beside an old steam engine, at that moment firing up its boiler and pouring forth a cloud of white steam
and coal smoke. Yes, there was even a coal car piled full behind the
engine, ready to drench the forest in soot. I knew why they were
there. Similarly, the three men I saw once while I was on a bicycle
ride. They stood on a bridge high in a mountain pass awaiting the
passage of a steam engine. They had their cameras and telephoto
lenses on tripods placed about the entire pass to photograph the
engine from many angles. It's suspicious if not outright illegal in
our post-9/11 world to do as those men were doing, but in that
last moment before violent history intruded on their reveries, they
basked in the world as it was, as it might again someday be: all of
us riding together, only a few sheepish-looking snobs in the limited first-class seats. Despite our differences, we're trying to figure
out how to make this trip together work out. In the meantime, as
we must wait for *that* train, which is very late, let us celebrate the
idea of a possibly better world.

A few days later, as we blew through Rottweil again, this time
on a regional express, I glimpsed another two boys standing on
the near platform, jumping up and down with pleasure as we
passed through the station. It's a pleasure I recognize. They are
waiting for someone they love. Of my own first experiences on
a train when I was those boys' age, I understand now it was the
same train on which my soon-to-be mother rode back to Wooster
College, six years earlier, after Thanksgiving of 1957. She had
spent the summer nights in the company of my soon-to-be father
and they had returned to that island in a nearby lake on which
they went water-skiing earlier in the year. They didn't know it yet,
but they would soon marry. Nor did she yet suspect that she was
pregnant, though she must have wondered if something hadn't
changed. My father would be alive for another five years. An almost unimaginably long time in an eighteen-year-old's life. The

trees in the hills south of Alliance had already dropped their leaves and the fields were in stubble. Frost lay on the pastureland. She must have ridden into that winter of her twentieth year in wonder. Soon, it would begin to snow. How alive and happy she must have felt.

THE DHARMA UPSTREAM

*Shariputra, all things are empty—not born, not destroyed, nei-
ther defiled nor pure, without loss, without gain.*

—THE HEART SUTRA

The landscape north of my hometown was an unlikely destination
for any of the weekly outings my grandfather and I took during
the 1960s. Dominated by shallow strip mines and a notoriously
polluted reservoir just ten miles downstream from steel mills, it
was countryside "hard on the eyes," my grandfather said as he
launched into a diatribe that deployed his preferred epithet: "goddamned *Swinus Americanus* have been here."

There existed, however, a didactic aspiration to these outings
greater than his disgust for litter and the benighted practices of
extractive industries. He took me once, for example, to the nineteenth-century fairgrounds on North Rockhill Road to discover
remnants of the horse track and lake. We could see the sandy track
beneath our feet, though it had returned to beech forest; the lake
was a mosquito-incubating puddle. This, like so much else in Alliance, Ohio, was the world of *his* childhood, the traces of which
had grown obscure, present in his memory but otherwise absent.
My grandfather wished to teach a lesson about the impoverish-

167

ments of our post-war boom, its devouring of natural resources, men, and memory, but his pupil took lessons in resilience. Don't give in to *Swinus Americanus*. Don't believe the ugliness of our town mirrors the permanent condition of your life or landscape of your memory and imagination. The present state of affairs is a contingency only. Stasis, an illusion. Someday, maybe, we will all come to our senses.

In the meantime, scrubby fields covered miles of countryside as far as the imaginal boundaries of my world. Growing over all those ruined places north of town, from collapsing tipples and mine timbers scattered throughout slag heaps to polluted streams bank to bank with orange sludge, there were also the ubiquitous poverty grass, sumac, trees of heaven, and blackberry brambles that had begun the slow succession of healing. If I looked closely, if I compared, I might draw the conclusions my grandfather intended: here are the kinds of solace life offers. The countryside wasn't so much a separate place, but the least hostile element of life itself, a life whose sole intention seemed to be toiling to close the wounds gouged upon it.

My grandfather enjoyed bicycling as much as rambling across fields and through forests, and in this, I followed his example. Injuries he received in a bicycling accident, however, were the likely cause of his death. He was pedaling south of Alliance on his maroon, five-speed Schwinn Suburban, intending to weed the garden he shared with his brother-in-law, William Henning, when a Vietnam vet lost his composure. He swerved his car into my grandfather, blindsiding him and leaving him lying in the barrow pit alongside a rural road. The doctor, a family friend, warned my grandfather to take it easy, let the blood clots dissolve before returning to normal activity. He ignored that advice and his own beliefs about the necessity of permitting things to heal. Days later a blood clot lodged in his heart as he mowed the lawn, his gesture of goodwill on Mother's Day, 1976.

One stifling afternoon in summer a decade earlier, we had ridden our bikes north of town on Union Avenue, crossed the Mahoning River, and passed through an entire landscape of mine tailings—gray heaps of brittle wafers of shale. Just before we reached the intersection with US 224, which would have led us farther downriver toward Youngstown, we turned east onto Fewtown Road and stopped at an overlook on a high cutbank above a backwater of Berlin Lake, formed when the Mahoning was dammed in 1942. We climbed off our bikes and walked them into the mottled shade of a honey locust grove. We looked out at what once had been a bottomland of forest and farm fields. The forest was by then a dense thicket of partly submerged, bare, gray tree trunks. Owing in no small part to its isolation and bleakness, that area has since become infamous for its association with a series of suspicious deaths, likely murders, that remain unsolved.

While we stood side by side in the shade, we saw something uncanny. In the distance, perched on the fallen trunks of dead trees just above the waterline, were creatures whose beauty was so foreign it was little more than a rumor, a vestige of a former world I had no knowledge of prior to that moment. I suspected that my grandfather knew these creatures were there all along and had only waited to show them to me when I was capable of enduring the ordeal of getting there on my own. The ordeal was a necessary part of the gift he wished to bestow.

"What are they?" I said.

"Herons," he said, and fished out an old pair of field glasses from the World War I gas mask bag he used to carry our sandwiches and water. "Look through the binocs," he said, handing them over.

The herons cocked their heads for a better look at us, it seemed. Their elegant black plumes curled behind their yellow eyes, and long gray plumes fanned out from their necks and chests. They remained so still that if I hadn't previously seen them tilt their heads, I would not have believed they were alive.

Soon, though, they began screeching *grak-grak*, and then startled up into the air. We watched them rise slowly, gaining altitude above the marsh. Their shadows moved beneath them across the water, and when we stepped out of the grove to watch them pass overhead, their shadows crossed our faces.

"What are they?" I asked again.

"Birds," he said. "Great blue herons."

ॐ

About the time my grandfather took me to meet the herons, I entered a bookstore for the first time.

The News Depot at the corner of Market Avenue and Second Street in downtown Canton, Ohio. It was the autumn of 1966. I was eight years old.

My memory is probably not very reliable, but I recall the News Depot as a genial place, with its plate-glass windows facing onto two streets, a large newspaper and magazine rack between rooms, and square display islands and bookshelves along the walls, fashioned from light, creamy maple, all covered with newly published books,. It seems brightly lit in my memory, though it was late afternoon, during a melancholy time of year.

Twenty miles to the east, Alliance, the town of twenty thousand (more or less) people in which I was born and reared, had no bookstore, except for the one in the Mount Union College student union, and so far as anyone knew, it sold only textbooks and Purple Raider sports paraphernalia. We drove to the nearest "big" town, as we did for many things in the 1960s that seemed more exotic than Alliance allowed: Kurosawa films, for example, or sandalwood incense, batik bedspreads, Ravi Shankar albums, and Constant Comment Tea, all of which were truly exotic, "Oriental," as I'm sure we said at the time. Books were no less foreign to our fellow citizens, though there was a bookcase in our house with a new Collier's encyclopedia and accompanying set of *The Junior Classics* from the series The Young Folks Shelf of Books.

In the News Depot that day I prevailed on my mother to purchase three books of my choosing. In 1966, I was pretty much still illiterate, despite the good intentions of Mrs. Stapleton and Mrs. Witherspoon, who tried to teach the phonics curriculum for the first and second grades at Rockhill Elementary School. That is where I was directed toward the permanent stain of "special class," and where, once liberated by my mother's howls of protest, I remained a sullen, sometimes disruptive, presence for the remaining five years of my primary education. All of which makes the books I chose that day more than a little odd.

These three estimable books, which I still have in my possession fifty years later, are the 1962 Pelican Original *Buddhism* by Christmas Humphreys, the 1951 New Directions edition of *Siddhartha* by Herman Hesse, and the Penguin Classics edition of *The Narrow Road to the Deep North and Other Travel Sketches* by Matsuō Bashō. They would likely have been shelved in different sections—religion and philosophy; fiction; and the notional category of extended education, cultural enrichment, and self-improvement once known as world classics, a project of post-war progressivism that my Young Folks Shelf of Books was, likewise, the product of.

⟿

Those two incidents from early in life were much on my mind last August when, after a slow, hot, and humid slog through plagues of flies, my constant companion and I pitched camp on the headwall of Nooksack Ridge in the North Cascades. As afternoon cooled into evening, we sat on an elephant-sized boulder and looked back down the long canyon we ascended earlier. We shared a bowlful of attitude-adjusting weed and passed a flask of bourbon, but soon it was clear that I had perhaps had a bit too much to dream.

Earlier, I'd dumped water over my head from my grandfather's canvas water bucket; the rim of the bucket had sealed over my scalp and it had the effect of holding my head inside a tub of ice. It's a foolish way to cool off a dehydrated, overheated body, and later, sitting on that rock, I could sort of feel myself slowly going into shock.

Josefa, meanwhile, was rhapsodizing beside me, recalling the moment in her own youth in Colorado when she first experienced the freedom of the mountains on the ridge of Arapaho Peak, as that day long ago, before I knew her, when she loved another man, darkened toward twilight and the first stars appeared. I think she may even have been softly singing a Neil Young song. I'm not sure, as I was crying, helpless myself, and her voice seemed far away.

The rock beneath me grew strangely malleable. I was sinking into it, in fact; I was by then *inside* the rock, trying not to panic, as death through the agency of elephant-sized rock at that moment closed over me, claiming whatever mineral resources my life amounted to for redistribution to other more viable life forms. It took all the focused energy I could muster to interrupt my constant companion's rhapsody and choke out, "I'm so sorry, I'm a bit of a mess just now."

Josefa stood far above me at the surface of the earth and extended her warm rough hand into the darkness below, retrieving me from that heavy, cold, but oddly molten substance in which I was drowning. She stood me up on my feet and led me from the rock through heather, elk sedge, and bracken ferns toward our tent. By this time, I'd broken out in a drenching sweat.

"Wait," I said, "I have to take the biggest piss ever," and soon unleashed a torrent onto the heather at my feet.

That's when things got weird.

All the plants in the meadow around me, the entire mountain-side, turned into a viscid, glowing green goo that rose to my knees and from which there was no way to extricate myself, even if I'd wanted to do so. It was kind of entrancing. Why was I typically unaware of this beautiful, vibrant goo? Then the green goo start-ed singing softly or humming, anyway, like a swarm of bees. "I'm going to be fine," I said, "I just need to lie down for a moment." And lying back in the sedge, I started narrating my hallucination.

～

Though it wasn't accompanying me that night on Nooksack Ridge, Bashō's *The Narrow Road to the Deep North* was the one book of the three my mother purchased for me at the News Depot in 1966 that I continued to carry in my pack into the wilderness as a younger man. Bashō's little book affirmed what my grandfather avowed was the-right-at-that-moment-narrowing path toward a continuation of an otherwise meaningful life. It begins at trail-heads and opens into the deep north.

That day in 1966 was only a few lateral moves from my first learning (during weekend peregrinations with my grandfather) to make a comfortable camp bed from the fallen needles of white pines, to learning finally to read, to "I have come a long way since I left my house . . . determined to become a weather-exposed skele-ton." I was at that very moment on Nooksack Ridge inadvertently getting a very personal glimpse of just such a skeleton. I didn't know whether to laugh or cry.

Similarly, it's only a few more lateral moves from chapters six through twelve and thirty through thirty-four of *The Dharma Bums*, which I read for the first time the winter *before* my grand-father died, to Colin Fletcher and *The Man Who Walked Through Time*, which I read the August I returned from my first hike on the Appalachian Trail *after* my grandfather died, to Gary Snyder's "Mid-August at Sourdough Mountain Lookout."

And it's still fewer lateral moves from standing in the clouds a decade or more ago on Gold Ridge in the Pasayten Wilderness (I may have been stoned then, too)—where, looking west as the clouds lifted, we could make out the Pacific Crest Trail a few miles away along the Devil's Backbone—to my hallucinations on Nooksack Ridge just west of there in August 2016.

Before I dumped ice-cold water onto my very overheated head, I'd searched for a campsite farther up the ridge than the one we eventually chose, hoping to catch a strong enough breeze off Ruth Mountain's glaciers to keep the black flies at bay. Shade and breeze I could find, but not water. Though we didn't make our camp in the grove of old trees with a grassy glade at its center, there in the clearing was a bed of pine boughs someone last autumn cut and carefully arranged. Over that bed of crisscross boughs that only in the previous week had emerged from snow, I knelt and heard my grandfather's name.

~◇~

Robert Peters was an unusual man, a bit screwy really, and absurdly funny, but also—there's no denying it—emotionally unstable, and because of this he never fostered close friendships with other more conventionally tuned men of his time and place. Compared to him, they seemed in stoic lockdown. Publicly anyway. Hot summer nights you could sometimes hear them coming unhinged within their own houses, from whence their wives seldom escaped. My grandfather was no stranger to their fury, though he would literally tremble at the thought of the emotional lock and key of mid-twentieth-century American masculinity, and therefore avoided being subjected to it whenever he could, because he sure couldn't avoid it at work, where, I gathered, if he wasn't bullied, he was certainly the source of others' merriment. Joyous spontaneity and a loving regard for exaggeration (a rhetorical form of exuberance) were the chief characteristics of his inner life.

Painful experience of the humiliating sort had taught him the social costs of his sudden hyperbolic flights of mind, which he gave full expression to only as we walked through the fields or forests of northeastern Ohio, or as we sat at fireside in our camp at night.

Hardly a week passed without our taking a day-long walk together; that is, if we weren't camping out over an entire weekend. Sometimes we met his brother-in-law, Phil Clark, and Phil's daughter, Becky, my first love. Uncle Phil was a much-decorated war hero who saw a lot of action in the theaters of war and suffered for it long into his late middle age, by which time he had withered into a bitter, conservative old man. Before that, though, whenever we met up, Phil and Becky would be miles from home, somewhere along Beech Creek playing on a sandbar, often in the cool shadows under the bridge at the bottom of Vine Street, where we would find them and continue together into the forests.

In other words, Robert Peters and his grandson were great pals, he filling in for my early-departed father. We remained in each other's constant presence until I became a teenager, and even then, though relations between us naturally grew strained, we weren't always absent of the other's company. The last we spoke in the early spring of 1976, he sweetly asked if I would like to go swim a mile with him at the Y. It was something we'd often done together since I turned nine and managed to swim my first uninterrupted mile. I declined, though I knew to do so was a little perverse. He died suddenly two months later. Since that shocking turn of events, which vividly recalled the not-so-distant demise of my young father, I felt chastened and ashamed of myself, and my grandfather soon was fully restored as the companion, in absentia, of my own inner life. During the last weekend I visited, home from my freshman year in college, he had begun to talk about planning a hike on the Appalachian Trail, the fulfillment of his lifelong dream to walk great distances in the forests and mountains of America's public lands. Two months after his death, I stepped onto the AT with a dear friend, and ever since I moved to the West, I've seldom let a week pass when I haven't hiked, bicycled, or skied in the mountains and forests near my home. Most weeks, I've swum at least a mile in his memory.

Robert Peters never strays far from my thoughts, particularly in the backcountry. Our third morning in the North Cascades, by then on Copper Ridge, Josefa, still bundled in her down jacket and gloves, commented that in the thirty-seven years she has known me, during which time we've walked and camped together throughout the mountains of the American West, she has never once heard me express anything but the deepest affection for the man. I was making breakfast as she made this declaration, and had just prior to this been chattering way, repeating, as I do when I'm especially happy, the catalogue of ridiculous shit that came out of his mouth whenever he was making a meal for us in the forests where we camped out, in pursuit of an imaginary world much vaster and less beleaguered than our heartbroken Ohio countryside.

"Num sareta voita frenyso, chefatche pina mo," served him in any and all circumstances. "Peewee wankum zooy, dushwuck-das do, yuckish mickafivish, mactavish, sanova beach dundee," or any isolate phrase within that string of nonsense indicated a state of being, a critical commentary, or agreement, whereas *sanova beach*, as in *Bossa Nova Beach*, was an actual place, sort of, the name given to an unofficial park along the Mahoning River where the races met with congenial rather than hostile intent, though it also served as a mild epithet, an equivalent of "I'll be shipped in dit."

More specific, but no less metaphoric, was the oddly imperative question, "Put the baby on it?" That is, would you like mustard on your Spam sandwich? Or in response to my saying that I was thirsty, a nominally innocent way of asking "what are you going to do about it," he answered with his own irony, "I'm Friday, glad to meet you." By which he meant only that my enunciation sounded moronic.

"Bug-juice?" he would ask. Bug-juice was a "suicide" mixture of whatever flavors of Hi-C or Hawaiian Punch (or store brands) were on sale and poured together into a milk can along with a ten-pound sack of sugar. Implied in the question was another question: "You really aren't going to complain about the flies in it, are you?" Another favorite saying of his, which I'm pretty sure he borrowed from Bob Elliot and Ray Goulding, was, "By god, that looks almost good enough to eat!" *That* would have been "Hungarian Hotpot," the soup that was, like bug-juice, an unabashed admixture of all soups available in cans, which he inevitably prepared while camping.

On that ridge in the North Cascades—where, as per usual, this silly litany spilled off my tongue, and where, once coffee, granola, and Astro Eggs had worked their magic on our gastrointestinal systems—I repeated with cheerful urgency my grandfather's most grandiloquent locution of all: "Good Lord, get a shingle and scrape your leg!" Josefa then sent a tremor through me when she added, "I wish I could have met him." Meaning she wished he could have hiked with us these past thirty years.

How I wish that, too! Or at least I wish she could meet the man he has become during these past four decades as I recreated him.

The glaciers on Mount Baker and Mount Shuksan gleamed just above our camp to the west, snow-clad mountain ridges and green river valleys receded as far as we could see to the north and south, and Mount Redoubt dominated the horizon just to our east. As I've aged, the only father I've ever known as my own, my mother's father, Robert Peters, has accompanied me, my Virgil, guiding me through this otherworld. And increasingly I see his eyes, and the emotional tenor of the inner life that he couldn't mask, reflected in my own eyes and expression. Growing a beard has done little to disguise the similarity. That tremor of tears Josefa sent through me was the same I felt in the months just after he died, when I walked the AT, and soon after, when I discovered James Wright's *Shall We Gather at the River*, in which Wright, in the poem "Youth," describes his own father who "toiled fifty years / At Hazel-Atlas Glass, / Caught among girders that smash the kneecaps." It reminded me of my grandfather returning home from a similar kind of work at the Alliance Machine Company, where he toiled as many years.

That quietude was indicative of our weekends tramping about the countryside, long hours of silence passing without a word between us. That silence was interrupted only by the ambient sound of Beaver Run or Beech Creek sluicing across sandy shoals; the wind in the limbs of beeches, maples, and elms; redwings trilling in the marshes; or our feet shuffling through leaves on the forest floor. There was peace to be found in the forest and at edges of fields, peace at least relative to the hazards of the factory floor or frustrations of matrimony. My grandfather was no Buddhist, let me tell you, but our rambles were undistorted by either desire or frustration, and I felt in no way delimited by the melancholy of home, where the grief of my father's death and my mother's running off continued to hang over us like a fog. Those forests and fields provided me with a solace I found nowhere else.

That solace was a physical sensation of the ample gratitude one feels toward this difficult life. It was, specifically, the embodiment of gratitude for a man I loved, without until that moment ever really having said so, least of all to myself, approaching the age now at which he died. He gave me this life—that moment on Copper Ridge and all those others that preceded it during the forty intervening years between his death and now. It was, in the thousand ways he transmitted it, a tremendously generous gift. It's as true now as ever, what Lewis Hyde wrote forty years ago in *The Gift*. Gifts must keep moving and changing hands.

◦

On a recent afternoon, walking near Dupont Circle in Washington, DC, my oldest son and I got caught in a thunderstorm and dashed across the circle into the Phillips Collection.

It so happened that in the rotunda of the gallery that day, Morris Graves's paintings hung in a circle all around us. Graves spent his early years not far from La Grande, Oregon, on a homestead in Fox Valley in rural Grant County. I first encountered Graves's work in my early thirties, specifically his painting of a ponderosa sapling, *Joyous Young Pine,* on the cover of Robert Aiken's *Mind of Clover.* Since that first encounter, I've sought out his work wherever I can find it in museums and galleries—Seattle, La Conner, Cleveland, Columbus—as well as in exhibition catalogues, such as *The Early Works* and *The Falcon of the Inner Eye.* Josefa and I once even arranged to publish a portfolio of his late flower paintings in the magazine we edited, *basalt.* Graves's vision has continued to deepen in me a sense of the hauntedness of the Pacific Northwest, the whole sensorium set ablaze with the spirit of this place. To seek out his paintings in museums and galleries is to stand at a portal and gaze deeper into the covert emotional landscapes of Oregon and Washington. I taste what Graves saw in the food I grow in rural Oregon.

Besides a brief return to the West Coast after completing his undergraduate degree, my son has lived the last decade along the Eastern Seaboard, where he works as an environmental policy analyst. Every year, he typically visits the Pacific Northwest once for work and once for pleasure. I know, however, he often checks the local webcam that looks out on Mount Emily, just north of La Grande, where he spent his youth. I am loathe to ask him if anything of that youth, much of it spent tramping around in wilderness areas of the Pacific Northwest, was transmitted to him as a fundamental element of his own being. Does his former familiarity with this vast and geographically diverse landscape still grow in his soul? Will it grow in his children's souls?

If I were to ask him those overheated questions, he would likely express his concern at my well-being and state of mind. And naturally, if my chauvinistic bias for the Pacific Northwest weren't equally an expression of my provincial anxieties, I could answer those questions reliably myself. His answer—or for that matter, his younger brother's answer if he were similarly queried—would be affirmative. The frenzy of their outdoor activities and gustatory pursuits whenever they return home is evidence.

What I wondered that day in the Phillips Collection was if my sons were in possession of any sense of their great-grandfather's presence in their lives. Had what my grandfather transmitted to me in Ohio long ago been successfully transmitted to them, who never met the man? Our sons were present for twenty-five of the forty years I described the man and the habits of his mind to Josefa, so it seems plausible that the transmission was successful. I hoped, as my grandfather hoped for me in our shared time and place, that my son would sense the native intelligence of his spiritual home in those very paintings. The paintings were, after all, the work of a man of my grandfather's generation. My grandfather, I think to his great sorrow, lacked the opportunity art lends to its makers to express themselves in a manner that exempts those they love from having to bear the burden of that exposure. That I guess is the golden knot of being: how to express our love without betraying the intimacy of that love.

I'm not certain my eldest was quite aware of what we were looking at or how it related to him, or that all these things roiled my mind at once and ever since. The whole North American continent and several lifetimes separated us at that moment from the places and occasions of those paintings, as those paintings and their maker were separated from the crimes that cleared that landscape of its first people and their abiding claims to it. Standing beside him, however, I felt as though we stood again as we had decades before near La Push, Washington, when we paused before *Wounded Gull*.

Among Graves's most famous and emotional works, *Wounded Gull* takes for its subject something anyone who has walked a Northwest beach has seen—a badly mangled, "common" bird. The painting is expressionist, however, the antithesis of an ornithological drawing. The setting is the beach at dusk, the natural light muted by clouds. Through banks of fog, there is a distant view of gunmetal seas, and in the upper left corner of the painting, just a glimpse of the sky reflected on gray open ocean at the horizon. Two wavering red bands of reflected sunlight appear as long diagonals on the darker water, one in the upper third of the painting above the gull, the other in the lower third, intersecting the gull. Those red lines also are in motion, being rolled under the blue surf, and are equally an expression of emotion for the gull, the tip of whose lower beak is daubed red, connecting reflected sunlight with blood.

It's the bird that held our attention. The rendering of the skeletal creature and the brutal conditions it faces alone is achieved in a few bold, painterly brushstrokes of blue and white. I had the sense of it being painted as quickly and assuredly as a classically trained Chinese calligrapher would render a mountainside, a pine, wildlife, or human beings in a few deft stokes. So immediate is the vulnerability Graves achieved, I felt that familiar tremor of tears beginning to rise through me as soon as I walked into the room. Graves saw more than that dab of blood on the bird's beak, its eyes clamped shut in pain. The gull's visible left foot twists one hundred-and-eighty degrees, so that it points the direction opposite the direction the bird faces. It's excruciating.

Graves painted *Wounded Gull* soon after his draft status as a World War II conscientious objector was resolved and he was released from the stockade at Fort Roberts. He was discharged and "returned to civilian life because of his inability to adapt to military service," writes Ray Kass in his essay that accompanies the exhibition catalogue for *Morris Graves: Vision of the Inner Eye*. Kass says of this painting that it "reflects Graves' despair from his military service," but also that it avoids "clichés of pathos and self-pity that one might expect from the subject matter." Surely this is true, but I wonder if there isn't something else here in the painting. Kass explains that *Wounded Gull* was painted on a camping trip to the Olympic Peninsula after Graves returned to his home on The Rock, that is, Fidalgo Island, across the Swinomish Channel from La Conner, Washington. And so, it seems my son and I were standing together, after all, somewhere between La Push and Cape Alva. If we felt something of the artist's despair, that is perhaps more complex than an expression of his personal circumstances, trying as they were. What I experience whenever I look at *Wounded Gull* is Graves's deep empathy for life, human or otherwise, a response heightened by wartime for sure, and completely in keeping with his pacifist and Buddhist views, a current of which has long existed in the Pacific Northwest. That is to say, I recognize the emotional tenor of our regional home, the ocean, shoreline, forested coastal ranges, and the diversity of lives found here.

Of the remainder of the paintings from the 1940s present in the gallery that day, with perhaps the exception of the atavistic symbolism of *Chalice*, all are related by time, place, temperament, and imagery to *Wounded Gull*. Those paintings—*Eagle, In the Night, Surf and Birds*, and *Sanderlings* (my favorite really, with its the tender and alert synchrony)—each is evocative of the ecology of the Pacific Northwest that my sons and I shared with their mother without interruption for twenty years.

Increasingly now, I regard work like Graves's as a conversation the artist is having not simply with a landscape, but with the ecological intelligence indigenous to the Pacific Northwest, its familiar seasonal surfaces and haunted substance. The work expresses the artist's gratitude for the moments of vision granted and the intelligence transmitted to him by the place not only in his time, and from the past, but also from our future, where the accretions of absence weigh us down in our tar-drenched clothes.

❧

We returned a month ago from backpacking up East Eagle Creek in the Wallowa Mountains with our youngest son, who was visiting from South America. During our walks together, he collected sounds from the mountains in which he had spent his youth—the evening air glimmering in aspens, creek water splashing through boulders, mule deer in our camp at night poking about with their noses and hooves for the boletes we picked and were drying, the sounds of water and wind meeting at a lakeshore, and, as the full moon rose along the ridge behind us one evening, the solitary voice of a great gray owl—the phantom of the north—calling at the edge of a meadow. Soon after his return to Cali, he began to integrate these samples into the ecologically based music he makes. Early in his process, he sent us a condensed and sped-up sound file of the entire weekend, which had an overpowering visceral effect on me. In thirty seconds of sound waves, pink frequencies heard in tides, beating hearts, and quasars, it expressed the entire physical and psychic tenor of that three-day trip.

One evening during our brief sojourn in the mountains together, I was tying off the bear bag full of food I'd slung across a branch high in a Douglas fir, and I realized my grandfather was standing there beside my son. Together, absent and present, visible and transparent, they watched as I tied the knot I always tie whenever I hang the bear bag or tighten the guylines of a tent or tarp in the wind.

"I want to see how you do that," my son said.

"It's a taut-line hitch." I said. "I learned it from my grandfather. You can tie it with a slip, like this." I made a loop with a bow instead of tying it off with a clove hitch. "That way you can untie it more quickly."

I undid the knot, but kept the tension in the line, then handed him the rope so he could try to tie the knot. Two turns inside the loop and a half-hitch outside.

"Dress it tight," I said, showing him how the knot will tighten as he shortened the rope.

❧

My grandfather was no Buddhist, though he achieved something like the transmission of dharma to me during our brief time together. Neither of us would have used that term, *dharma*, when I was a little boy, but it was certainly in those three books my mother bought her illiterate son fifty years ago. By the time my grandfather died ten years later, I had stumbled on *The Dharma Bums* and its corollary Rucksack Revolution, of which, if I wasn't a card-carrying, I was surely a backpack-carrying, member. I had read the story of Jack Kerouac blurting out to D. T. Suzuki when they met in New York the summer before I was born, "Why did Bodhidharma come from the West?" My grandfather had crossed his own great distances with tremendous difficulty to share "something here, Axeldragon, that will interest you."

Our outings over the years were generally more mundane than that day my grandfather introduced me to herons. The period during which I came of age—the late sixties and early seventies—were famously turbulent, nowhere more so than in our household, where my grandfather witnessed on television a world that seemed to have betrayed everything he believed in. Many of us experience the same confusion when we realize that what we presume to be true, stable, known, and world-making can no longer taken for granted. It seems inevitable that an elderly man

who came of age in the late 1920s would find himself in conflict
with a boy who felt passionate about the causes of his own youth.
Our outings therefore became less frequent. I often went alone
once I was old enough to do so, resuming the lonely wandering I
enjoyed even earlier, when I was still living in my mother's household and could disappear into forests, marshes, and farm fields
without being missed.

During the same visit when I declined to join him at the pool,
we decided to spend a morning together, searching for the source
of the Mahoning River. That the river had several branches was of
no consequence to our plan. We agreed that the river's true source
was likely above a low marshy area, Beaver Run, in the rolling hills
ten miles south of town, where we often went on outings and did
trail work at Camp Limrod, named in honor of a wealthy donor
and Presbyterian congregant, Lily M. Rodman, whose family
name was also on the local library and observatory.

Here, as elsewhere, mining had distorted the landscape. A
strip mine operated on the north side of the Beaver Run Valley,
and we watched summer nights in the latter half of the 1960s
from a hillside across that valley as machinery waded through
the floodlit pit. One evening we brought along a small telescope
and tripod to look at Jupiter's moons and the craters on Earth's
own moon, but inevitably, we turned the barrel toward the pit,
where we observed the shovel scoop up the sulfurous coal and
dump it into Leviathan-sized trucks with wheels as tall as a man.
Little we suspected that we were all burning a hole through our
world.

After the mine played out, a deep emerald pool of contami-
nated water that coal mining companies call "sweet water" filled
the pit. We dutifully volunteered to replant the spoil banks
with white pine and birch. Where a forest had once grown and
was destroyed, we opened holes in the tailings with Pulaskis,
reached for one of those tiny trees we hauled around in damp

canvas sacks on our hips, shoved the hairy roots into the hole, and with our boot heels closed the holes. Then I fetched a bucket of creek water, polluted by the heavy metals leeching from the pit, which my grandfather dumped onto the seedlings, and then I ran after another.

Something like a forest grows today over those spoil banks, which provides no small satisfaction. The trees add a layer of leaves, needles, and humus every year, which someday, maybe, will renew a place coal mining ruined. That forest, such as it is, provides the truest glimpse into my grandfather's mind.

The hills just south of the mines where we often walked remained an unmolested upland forest of beech, maple, oak, and elm, which gives way to sycamore and willow, then to the broad expanse of marshy ground through which Beaver Run meandered. The marshes were often loud with birdsong and chorusing frogs. We wandered together there year-round when I first moved into my grandparents' household. We camped on the forested ridge, hiked to the marshes at dusk, or sat on a hillside above the marshes as night rose from the valley, engulfing us in a broad shadow. Soon, the stars wheeled above, while below will-o'-the-wisp throbbed. Whenever we hiked back through the forest to our campsite in the dark, we followed a trail that mirrored the sky, the ground at our feet lit by pale coals of phosphorescence. Years later, standing in a chaotic bookstore in Evanston, Illinois, I burst open again with recognition when that same image of phosphorescence appeared at the end of Kenneth Rexroth's famous poem "Signature of All Things."

My grandfather and I often walked at Beaver Run on the weekends whenever my grandfather suffered "the fistariss." What he suffered from was fatigue and insult. His first and favored life mostly obliterated, he suffered in exile from the woman who rejected him, but who I think he must have loved, despite their grievances. In that area around Beaver Run, he saw time unfolding around him as he preferred to see it—past, present, and maybe a future that was and wasn't his, but surely was mine. There must have been some consolation in that. Perhaps that is why we love and try our best to foster the lives of the young, to glimpse life beyond the horizons of our own.

We walked through thickets impinging on old fields, high-canopied forests, and then the deep black silt of the marshes, where ten thousand creatures sang our praises throughout the spring and early summer mornings—a sanctuary of redwing blackbirds, great blue herons, kingfishers, Baltimore orioles, killdeer, marsh hawks, and myriad others. There were still beaver, muskrats, skunks, and a few deer living in the marshes then. Besides us, there were no other humans.

Our last day together before I left for spring term, we climbed the rocks to the top of a small mine at the head of the valley, where in winter we sometimes found the carcasses of cows that had wandered onto the ice and drowned when the ice broke beneath them. But it was early spring that day, and the carcasses had long since sunk to the bottom, where their bones collected in the layers of orange muck accumulating above them. We slipped around the cliffs above the pit, crossed a fence, and picked our way along a stream toward the source of the water that filled that valley and flowed north to join the river, eventually flowing through the industrial brown fields of Lower Alliance, and farther still, toward the heron rookery we visited a decade before. We continued to climb toward a ridge just below which we found the place where the stream rose from a crack in yellow sandstone. Moss clung to the rock. Under a canopy of honey locusts, spring beauties covered the ground. In the tiny stone pool below the spring, there was another layer of orange sludge. I asked my grandfather, "Shall I drink it?"

He thought a while, rubbing his stubbly chin. "No," he said. We stood then and watched it flow out of the ground, pool, then pour down the rocks into the broad valley full of rushes and singing birds. "Maybe just a little would be OK," he said, and we each dipped a handful and sipped.

"It's cold." I said. "It tastes like nothing at all."

AS THE WORLD CAUGHT FIRE

When Miranda and Prospero enter from the storm in the first act of *The Tempest,* Miranda suspects that her father is responsible for conjuring the storm that battered the ship just off the coast of their remote island. "If by your art, my dearest father, you have / Put the wild waters in this roar, allay them." By *art,* Miranda means *science,* for her father is no medieval conjurer, but a thoroughly modern man, poised at the brink of European modernity. His response to her sounds only too familiar to us, hearing it now at the end of the same era. "Be collected," he assures her, "No more amazement. Tell your piteous heart / There's no harm done." His condescension toward his daughter's "piteous heart" is less reassuring to us today than perhaps it was to his creator.

Later, as Prospero recounts their former lives, Miranda asks her father, "What seest thou else / In the dark backward and abysm of time?" She poses that question to her father at the threshold of the era of colonial expansion and capital accumulation, topics very much at the center of *The Tempest* and its concerns. According to NASA (National Aeronautics and Space Administration), the earth is now at another threshold: 407.62 parts per million of carbon dioxide, 1.8 degree Fahrenheit increase in global tem-

189

perature since 1880, 13.2 percent decline in minimum ice during the Arctic summer, a 286 gigatonnes per year decline in land ice, and a seven-inch rise in sea level over the past one hundred years. What else, we might also ask ourselves, do we see of our former lives, receding "In the dark backward and abysm of time?"

~o~

Looking over my own shoulder, I see the weird beauty of icebergs appearing off the North Atlantic coast this past spring—as many as four-hundred fifty—and feel resonant absence of a former world. In one foreshortened image taken with a telephoto lens, a translucent blue iceberg towers eerily above sightseers on a headland near Ferryland, Newfoundland. For thousands of years, our forebears must have gathered to stare in awestruck wonder whenever one of these wanderers appeared near the coast, a visitor from mythic Hyperborea.

Though icebergs are common enough in the subarctic, climatologists report that unusually strong winds drove a larger-than-normal number south from the tidewater glaciers of western Greenland. We don't need to be reminded today that weakening glacier ice has calved these rovers, and that the new severity of low pressure systems in the North Atlantic are regional manifestations of the acceleration of global warming at higher latitudes.

These recent visitors recall the anonymous Old English riddle I read when I first arrived in Montana. Roughly translated it goes:

> An exceptional being moved over the waves, attractive from
> its keel up. It called out in a loud voice. Its laughter was terrible,
> fearful to us on land. Its edges sharp, it was hate-grim, slow to be
> sated, bitter in warcraft. Hard and ravaging, it dug into shield-
> like hulls. Bound by hate-runes, it spoke with craft about its own
> making: "My mother is a powerful woman and she is my dear

daughter, grown upright, known among the sons of men and all
living beings, among whom she stands tall in her beauty."

The poem is formally interesting because it's a two-voiced riddle one within another, the first part focused on the threat of damage to seafaring vessels caused by the iceberg, which evokes the imagery of intractable combat. Insofar as seafaring and warfare are masculine domains, the fiercely female iceberg presents a hostile set of limitations on the prerogatives of commerce and raiding—*calm your piteous hearts!* The latter part of the poem is unequivocally an expression of female prerogative and is an elaborate conceit describing the water cycle. If the first part of the riddle challenges mercantile economies, the latter part is a reminder of more complex relations than those created by maritime commerce and its violent metaphors. The second riddle, spoken in a female voice by the iceberg itself, is a playfully paradoxical but closely observed expression of a related ecological phenomenon, the broader category of a large system essential to life. The iceberg is "calved" from snow and ice, but as it melts it evaporates and falls again as snow. The second part of this poem dramatizes how beholden we are to the very stable ecological processes that contain and sustain our household, and that we've subsequently undermined.

Such ecological processes are a world-making reality we all share, regardless of ideological prejudice or outright denial. If we're ever inclined to give it a thought, these recent appearances of icebergs evoke how much our situation has changed over the last several hundred years of the millennium separating us from this former iceberg's poet. This poem makes clear that awareness of ecological change is hardly restricted to human beings. In the imaginal space created by this riddle, regional climate itself finds a lyric voice.

❖

We now know the dispiriting consequences of Prospero's "art"—
we're living it. We're bombarded daily by evidence, whether of
famine, mass migration of whole populations, encroaching tides,
annual five-hundred-year floods, a fire "season" that now lasts
year-round, or a "continental-scale rearrangement" of river flows
in the Yukon. From the lede in *The Guardian*:

An immense river that flowed from one of Canada's largest
glaciers vanished over the course of four days last year, scientists
have reported, in an unsettling illustration of how global warming
dramatically changes the world's geography.

The river that disappeared was the Slim's. "For hundreds of
years," the article continues,

the Slim's carried meltwater northwards from the vast Kas-
kawulsh glacier in Canada's Yukon territory into the Kluane river,
then into the Yukon river towards the Bering Sea. But in spring
2016, a period of intense melting of the glacier meant the drainage gradient was tipped in favor of a second river, redirecting the
meltwater to the Gulf of Alaska, thousands of miles from its original destination.

This report stunned me, as "At Slim's River" was a lyric poem
that meant a great deal to me long ago as a student, just-arrived
in Montana, and already dreaming of the north. It's not perhaps
one of John Haines's finest lyrics, but its formal movement shifts
through his familiar concerns, summoning imaginal worlds of
absences and spectral futures that have ever since fascinated and
taught me to see. Haines stares steadily into the land. Much of
the poem's emotion is understated, as in the poet's nod to his
age, forty-nine being a meaningful threshold of its own in the unfolding of a human life. Haines steadily observes what is present
in the moment, and not just at the surface of things, but in their
depths of absence as well. He records all this in his direct, plain-
spoken voice. The ecology of this poem accounts for the stable
patterns and broad categories of relations the poet perceives in

the land—the grassy bluff, the wind, red rocks, the seasons and sun returning north, the vastness of the Yukon, and its "keen silence"—contrasted with the spectral brevity of human presence in that landscape. That constellation of phenomena greater and older than the human presence along Slim's River have the loudest voice—they make an ambient roar—in this otherwise soft-spoken poem.

I trust Haines's art instinctively, but not Prospero's. From that bluff, the poet gazes into the rapidly receding Holocene and Pleistocene. There's little reason to believe the poet is unaware of the consequences of the colonial world Prospero was a booster for in its infancy, what we since have come to call the Anthropocene. It intrudes, after all, at that dusty crossing where the clatter of modern machinery roars past in the distance. The poet doesn't quite know he's already entered our era, that the Holocene has ended, though it's likely that he senses it even in that wilderness; that is, Haines knew intuitively what is foremost in our minds today when we read this poem in an era of global warming.

Haines, like Robinson Jeffers before him, certainly was aware of the inevitability of human extinction, as he was of the post-war acceleration toward that reckoning. It's certainly a part of Haines's imagination, what was for Jeffers an outright longing for the end. The melancholy of the poem finds its source in reading the signs of that inevitability, but ultimately, it's a personal extinction the artifact of the poem attempts to countervail, not the disappearance of entire species.

Given the poet's meditation on varying scales of time in "At Slim's River"—the puniness of the human scale ("Alexander Clark Fisher. / Born October 1870. Died January 1941"), the vastness of geological time "a keen silence behind" all the poet sees, and the autotelic absorption in the living moment the little girl experiences who "had found a rock to keep"—the subsequent disappearance of Slim's River is shocking. In light of the erasure of the ecology from which the poem unfolded, the necessity of an ecological lyric such as Haines wrote throughout most of his life is more urgent than ever. With its keen eye for detail and intuitive awareness of symbiosis among different kinds of sentient presences within a habitat's past, present, and future, "At Slim's River" gives voice to the lives of others that we, who dwell in the Anthropocene with them, relentlessly silence or otherwise ignore to our mutual peril.

~&~

Looking over my own shoulder again into the abysm of time, I recall the gift a friend gave to me before he became a monk and took a vow of silence forty-two years ago. *A Dictionary of Symbols* by J. E. Cirlot, published in English translation by the Philosophical Library in 1962, has remained close at hand since the summer of 1976, by which time a dream of the north—fueled by Knut Hamsun's novels—had taken hold of me. One entry from that dictionary, under "Orientation," has long haunted me: "To face north is to pose a question." Apparently Etruscan soothsayers would orient themselves toward the north, that is, toward "the abode of the gods." It always struck me as obscure, though, as I tended to ignore or forget its context. I preferred that it mean something weirder: simply by facing north one poses a question.

Though I've never been any farther north than the boreal verge of the Arctic, my imaginal life has long oriented itself in that direction. Here in this tiny room in eastern Oregon, I look out along the valley, the ridges of the Blue and Wallowa Mountains vanishing over the curve of the earth into the north. If I could follow my gaze northward across that horizon, I would arrive eventually at the Columbia Wetlands, headwaters of the Columbia River. Having traced the trail of recessional glaciers through broad u-shaped valleys, marshes, and lakes, and climbed to the edge of the rapidly dwindling icefields of the Canadian Rockies, I don't know what question I could pose that wasn't elegiac, grief-stricken, full of longing for what will never return. My constant companion and I have paddled down a milky, glacier-fed river that emptied into a long narrow lake and slept under the shelter of old cedars grown from the receded glacier's moraines, the forest floor a foot deep in lichen and moss, the glacial chill still radiating from the earth—and the intimacy of our isolation was almost too much to bear. The world the north made possible downstream is dwindling away also.

Uncanny as it may seem, the climate, a river, or any other living thing affected by a warming climate can and does voice its awareness of the global fever at a similarly imaginal threshold. We're saturated with imagery of human ruin and planetary demise, and yet we seem curiously sanguine in our unwillingness to change the trajectory of our desires. What might change if we were better able to imagine how the rest of life—that is, ninety-nine percent of all life on the planet—is expressing itself in response to the same ecological stresses? That inability to pay closer attention is certainly not without consequences. I walked home after teaching one afternoon last winter accompanied by a colleague who teaches botany and has spent her life working to restore our local wetlands. We discussed amphibians and mass extinction. Acknowledging that amphibians worldwide are in steep decline, she reminded me that they have survived four of the five previous mass extinctions. "Theirs is among the oldest DNA," she said. I think she was suggesting that if amphibians, who are so adaptable that they have survived extreme periods of ecological unravelling such as we're in now, are at risk, then what kind of trouble are we in, who have never faced this ourselves? How long until a subsequent human generation recognizes its own imminent extinction not as an imaginary but as an ongoing event? Will languages then possess a future tense, and if so, will it be haunted by future absence? If our descendants still write poems, for whom will they imagine they write their poems? Does anyone alive today imagine those facing imminent erasure sifting through our litter to read our words? If they do, what will they find there that is of any use to them? Will elegy be the single affective register of our art?

Camille Seaman strikes an elegiac tone in her artist's statement in *The Last Iceberg*, a selection of eerie photographs from a larger body of her work, "Melting Away." "All things move toward their end," she writes, quoting Nick Cave. Trapped in its own time, an iceberg's absence is imminent in ours. Seaman's photographs may be an elegy to a colder world, but there is also an ontological urgency in her work that's expressive of an older, radical-seeming order that opens from precisely detailed observation toward metaphor, the bond of coequal being.

> Icebergs give the impression of doing just that [moving toward their end], in their individual way, much as humans do; they have been created of unique conditions and shaped by their environments to live a brief life in a manner solely their own. . . . I approach the images of icebergs as portraits of individuals, much like family photos of my ancestors. I seek a moment in their life in which they convey their unique personality . . . and a glimpse of their soul which endures.

There are elegiac examples throughout *The Last Iceberg*, like "Crumbling Iceberg I, Cape Adare," that possesses all of the eerie decrepitude of a phantom ship adrift in hyperboreal (or in this case hyper-austral) waters. Distant, sunlit mountains and tideline glaciers appear through a thin vapor. The ragged iceberg itself is in sharp focus and fills the middle third of the vertical and two-thirds of the horizontal composition. This otherworldly *Totenschiff* is surrounded by still gray, reflective water, in which both world and self mirror each other in decline.

Two images in particular, however, belie this elegiac tone and achieve a greater resonance. "Three Penguins in a Blizzard" is anti-nature photography at its finest. The horizon at the middle of the image could be miles away, it's hard to say. The sky that fills the upper half of the image is only a shade of white brighter than the pack ice below it. At the center of the image are at least a half-dozen icebergs frozen in place. Without the texture provided by the icebergs at the middle of the composition, the photograph would be a color field abstraction. The penguins are three small dots of black just right of center, toiling, so it appears, against the wind.

Contrast that to "Walking to the Iceberg, Cape Washington." The objects in the previous image were perceived at eye-level; here, those similar objects, observed under fair skies, are seen from an elevated position. The shades of white also tend more toward chromatic blues. Seaman adds a note: "After a blizzard tourists walk on the frozen Ross Sea to a giant [tabular] iceberg. The iceberg is over 2km away and in the deep snow it takes thirty minutes to reach it." Though the trail to the soaring iceberg is well trod by tourists in red parkas, it's the enormity of the sky, sea, and its pack ice that reminds us that there is a scale at which human beings and penguins (each species with their own predicaments) are virtually indistinguishable spectral presences. Our purposes, like our futures, perhaps as coequally certain as they are obscure in the moment.

Seaman's two images of "Where the Ice Should Be" further document the northward recessional memory of ice, and eerily echo Inupiaq poet Joan Naviyuk Kane's powerfully melancholic poem, "A Few Lines for Jordin Tootoo," in which she reflects on being in a lecture hall in Barrow, watching the pack ice open many months early. Kane listens to a discussion of "the old ways," the expectations that relearning a language returns the world to its older, more durable conditions. Or doesn't. Even more explicitly than John Haines before her, Kane senses the varying scales of time, self, and others in the arctic: ". . . what I hold within / is the felt absence of place. A land of great / failure, abundance: it goes on without us."

How does one cultivate the old ways that result "in little suffering or loss," as the forces that displaced the old ways undermine the very ecology from which the old ways emerged? Under such stress as this poem expresses, how will we ever restore the world we've lost or manage even to go on singing of that loss to the future, our dream of the possible? The poem refuses to offer any reassurances.

In the score of her composition *In the Light of Air*, Icelandic composer Anna Thorvaldsdottir instructs musicians to play "with calm & ease and a subtle sense of brokenness." Her music creates swirling, immersive ecologies of spectral sounds—bowing, for instance, the tone plates of a glockenspiel, as though they were cello strings, in her composition for four percussionists, "Aura." Listening to Thorvaldsdottir is like listening to a lava field dreaming about its grasses, migratory birds, fair weather cumulus clouds as their shadows sweep away to the east over gunmetal seas. When we look over our shoulders into the "abysm of time," we recognize how the poverty of Prospero's imagination brought us to this pass. If all we have now is what is in front of us, then truly, "a subtle sense of brokenness" seems a likely place from which our songs to the future might yet emerge and go on without us.

WHAT DOES THE WHITEBARK PINE SAY?

Fire season seemed mostly typical here in Oregon last summer. When the heat and wind arrived in July, the red flag warnings soon followed. We took back roads to Portland one day early in July with our son, driving on the north side of the Columbia River along the mostly continuous high ridge that separates the Columbia and Yakima Rivers, then across the southern flank of Mount Adams and its renowned huckleberry fields. Above the vineyards and orchards near Prosser, Washington, the tall spring grasses on the otherwise bare hills were, as usual, bleached tinder dry by sun and wind, as was the endangered prairie-oak savannah that dots the ridgetop and descends to the south between The Dalles and Hood River, Oregon. From that high ridge we could take in one of the most visually striking geographic areas of the Pacific Northwest—aligning with the snowcapped Cascade volcanoes Adams, Rainier, Glacier Peak, and Mount Baker to the north and Mount Hood to the south, looming over the gorge that the great Lake Missoula Floods scoured as the end of the last Ice Age began twelve thousand years ago.

Fires were already burning around the northwest, turning the sky vermillion at twilight and a perpetual reddish-brown throughout the day. A slight change in wind direction would fill the Grande Ronde Valley with thick smoke, and we'd have to keep the windows of our house closed despite the hundred-degree temperatures. In many ways, it's what we've come to expect. We dread its arrival. Then in September, a teenage boy threw a firework into the dry brush below a trail, starting the Eagle Creek Fire in the Columbia River Gorge. The subsequent wildfire exploded, and closures and evacuations soon followed, as the fire front burned to the edges of the Bull Run watershed, the water source for the city of Portland. By the time the fire was contained three months later, it had burned almost fifty thousand acres.

Whenever I think of how the native peoples of our region, whose traditional lives seemed somehow an offense to the moral conditions of modernity, and were dispossessed of this land as a result, it's hard not to wonder if those moral conditions of modernity—the causes of global warming— are so harsh that we who usurped a world from others are now being dispossessed of it, too. We are reminded daily that what we have done to others we have done to ourselves. There is no schadenfreude or comeuppance in this recognition of our cruel folly. We were never exempt from the consequences of our actions. We have condemned everyone to the same fate. Even after a winter of rain and snow, hotspots continued to smolder within the perimeter of the Eagle Creek Fire as late as May of the year after the fire started.

It had been a difficult summer for my constant companion and I, during which old quarrels and darker self-doubts occupied our thoughts, exacerbated by the awareness, as we age, that life feels increasingly done with us and that we stand in the way of the young whose anger about their future seems directed at our generation, who came of age in a more generous, egalitarian era. We felt deeply unsettled by this and wondered how directly our private struggles and the open hostility we sometimes felt were related to fire season, a symptom of global warming. We felt so paralyzed by the tetchiness in ourselves and others, we could hardly leave the house without a sense of dread following us into the streets.

It wasn't until late summer that Josefa and I finally left the household and hiked into the nearby Wallowa Mountains, wandering aimlessly in the forests, meadows, basins, and high ridges between nine-thousand-foot peaks in the eastern part of the Eagle Cap Wilderness. There's no alpine lake in that particular area, only a shallow stream, and therefore it fails to meet the requisite scenic criteria for a typical alpine outing. Fewer hikers select it, therefore, as a destination, and because we wandered so far afield, we seldom met anyone on these rambles besides a few local hunters, scouting for game in the weeks prior to the opening of hunting season.

The first night was clear enough that we could look up from our planet that caught fire through thin, red layers of smoke and gaze twenty-six-thousand light years through time and space all the way along the galactic plane toward the center of our galaxy, which intervening clouds of galactic dust obscure. That center is occupied by a swirling black hole whose massive gravity set the entire galaxy into motion. All our lives, we've orbited that galactic center together, everywhere around us invisible particles and waves becoming a glacier that carved the basin we camped in and where now the glacier has disappeared, turned into the water flowing past us in the stream. Particles and waves became cockleburs that snag in wool, the visible planets strung like beads along the ecliptic, a grove of fir trees, or the sound a grouse's wings made as it landed in the nearby grove.

The following morning, we crossed the creek we camped alongside and began our aimless wandering through lodgepole and fir forests. Those forests are interspersed with broad boggy meadows that in late summer are still full of blossoming geum, elephant head, and thick sedges. We made our way along the edges of the bogs, climbing slowly, and then through a steep boulder field that opened into a basin whose north face still lay deep in snow, the surface of the snow melting into waves blotched red by lichen. Josefa kept quiet and apart as we climbed that precarious boulder field, wrestling with her private thoughts, and wandered off alone into the basin among the bumblebee-laden flowers and sedges that had grown over and around the glacial till. Then we were side by side again, ascending another steep slope toward nine thousand feet, passing through groves of whitebark pines. "Will we ever become people again," she asked me, "like the whitebark pines?"

Maybe it was the elevation or the exposure, but I felt the surging vertigo of recognition rising through me in response to that question. If we'd climbed in isolation, we stood together now in intimacy with, and in relation to, all that lived around us. Those trees that grow only there under the harshest of conditions, and the particular species of bird, the Clark's nutcracker, that cooperates with the whitebark pine, are now under threat of extinction due to global warming. Ghost forests of whitebark pines haunt the high country, their trunks stripped of bark, the exposed sapwood glowing in groves turned dull silver. The trees that remain alive are often situated in groves already turning brown from the fungus that is killing them.

The Polish poet Adam Zagajewski, writing in his collection of essays *A Defense of Ardor* about another Polish poet, Zbigniew Herbert, makes a point of praising ". . . empathy, an unpopular aesthetic quality nowadays—*Einfühlung*, as certain neglected nineteenth century German philosophers would say—becomes the underpinning of his [Herbert's] art: tenderness toward the world, sympathy for both the major and minor players in the cosmos. 'Don't be surprised that we can't describe the world,' [Herbert wrote in his poem "Never About You"] 'we just speak to things tenderly by name.'"

Einfühlung. Tenderness toward being. That's what we felt, as well as the urge to speaking to things tenderly by name. I struggle to find something lacking in this position, especially as an ethics for how to conduct one's life toward others.

After a difficult summer, we were becoming more like people again on that ridge among trees who have lived centuries in that place and were happy we'd come to visit them. Later, as we descended, we visited with the sphinx moths sipping from the finitude of particular things—groundsel and buckwheat, monkeyflower glowing below a spring, late blossoming paintbrush. All our lives we've orbited with others whose names we've never learned, much less spoken tenderly, moving in all that time not so much as a degree of rotation along Orion's spiraling arm of the galaxy. Nor until later that evening, sitting near the creek, and just after Josefa brushed through flowering sage, had I ever tasted such sweetness in darkening air.

⌖

"In a world that seems increasingly focused on the needs of humans," Melissa Kwasny writes in *Earth-Recitals: Essays on Image and Vision*, "when plants and animals are dying out at an alarming rate, the struggle to widen the world to one where we exist *in relation to* other forms of life seems crucial." The biologist David George Haskill echoes Kwasny in a recent interview in *The Atlantic*. "The fundamental nature of life," he said, "may be not atomistic but relational." If they are correct, such a recognition would be an indispensable feature of the expression of tenderness toward being.

I can think of no gentler expression of this than John Cage's most famous composition, 4′33″. It's easily characterized as a prank, something not to be taken too seriously, ridiculed for its failure to confirm normative notions about what music, like obscenity, is. I can't define music, a critic of Cage might say, but I recognize it when I hear it, and Hayden's returning reliably to the tonic, *that's* music. In an article from the *New York Times* on the commemoration of Cage's seventy-fifth birthday, his music and audience are simple caricatures easily condescended to:

> There are some, to be sure, who find the very gentleness of Mr. Cage's [a]esthetic deeply appealing. For them, his sweet refusal to impose on a listener is a balm to the soul after the pushy insistence of most other music. Ultimately, these records serve the same function as Mr. Cage's essays, if not quite so eloquently. By receding deferentially into the background, they encourage, beyond indifference, a meditative concentration, which then quickly laps outward from the mere music to include the surrounding sounds: street noise, humidifier hum, phones ringing or, if one is listening in an acoustically sealed environment, one's own heartbeat, circulation and breathing.

The problem here is that gentleness, sweetness, and an unwillingness to impose one's self upon others in a shared space are easily dismissed as not serious. Just read the more eloquent essays, this judgement advises; at least that way you'll hear your own voice in your head.

Cage's gentle deference to others seems profound—a conceptual remedy to our catastrophic modernity that's careening toward its endgame. Those four minutes and thirty-three seconds of silence, in which the "music," an intentional object, accommodates itself to ambient sound, is an early expression of a developing ecological awareness that pervades music today.

His critics' skepticism notwithstanding, Cage's musical influence has only deepened and broadened since his death in 1992. Our household is often drenched in the performances of these immersive soundscapes, a lyricism that's derived from the music's relation to ambient presence. I hear it in Morton Feldman's sustained tones, or in Meredith Monk's diverse vocal sounds that engage in a call and response with fractal patterns, with coyotes, with silence itself. Listening to Monk at dusk with the windows open in summer, the screech owls fly closer to the house and the crows come to roost, fall silent, and listen to her sing. It's hard to deny the benevolent presence of Cage in such music's conception. Acknowledging this attentiveness to ambience opens attention toward nonhuman presences that surround us and is a clear expression of tenderness toward the diversity of being. One Waldelweiser composition I listen to often, *abgemalt* by Eva-Maria Houben, requires the greatest restraint. The pianist strikes a note and must allow it to decay to silence, during which interval ambient sound enters the music, such as the rain falling on the panels of the porch roof as I listen to the music accommodate itself to the ecology of my household this afternoon, the piano and rain balanced for a moment as one tone fades and the other brightens.

Such ecological lyricism, however, not only extends Cage's opening toward ambient presences, it traces those presences along the fungal-like networks of awareness among species, kingdoms of life, and the planet itself. In his journal on the composition of *The Place Where We Go to Listen*, an installation that transforms data collected from geomagnetic, seismological, and meteorological sensors in the region around Fairbanks, Alaska, into what the composer calls "An Ecology of Sound and Light," John Luther Adams writes that one of his principal motivations in creating *The Place* was the desire "to live ever closer to the earth, with a deeper awareness of the sentience all around me." As the composition evolves, Adams observes this about his desires and the achievement of the work itself:

> I've long said that I want the music to be larger than I am, richer and more complex than I can fathom, that I want to get lost in the music. Maybe in *The Place* this has finally happened. Maybe this piece can never belong to me. Maybe I

must learn to belong to it. I thought I had composed it. But it seems that it may have composed *me*.

In Adams's composition, we recognize the symbiotic or syncretic nature of what Kwasny called the crucial awareness: "we exist *in relation to* other forms of life." What is ingenious about *The Place* is how Adams has successfully imagined a way to translate the Earth's own music into a recognizable language of ambient light and tones, much of it otherwise inaudible to the human ear, invisible to the eye, while also accounting for the relational effect of the phases of the moon and aurorae interacting with the earth.

Timothy Morton makes a similar point about relational effects in *Humankind: Solidarity with Non-Human People* when he argues for the "subscendence-into-many," as opposed to the more familiar formula of transcendence into one. "Subscendence" is the recognition that the truism the whole is greater than the parts "is one of the most profound inhibitors of world-sharing." The term "world-sharing" we might define as the *opposite* of what E. O. Wilson calls "Anthropocene worldview": "the belief that all life should be henceforth valuated primarily or even solely for its importance to human welfare. In its extreme form, the worldview envisions future Earth as entirely enveloped and engineered by humans."

The truism, Morton argues, is "a symptom of agricultural-age monotheism," and Wilson's dystopian Anthropocene is, like capitalism, the logical outcome of agricultural-age monotheism, in which we become the image of a unitary God—the desert that trails civilization.

Our belief in our own exceptionalism, our standing apart from rather than as a part of the living world, however, is "haunted." Morton reminds us that from our gut to our skin, the human being is an amalgam of bacteria, viruses, and microorganisms, living symbiotically—that is, relationally—with the 10 percent of our cells that might be accurately categorized as strictly "human."

We're each of us composed, literally, of trillions of other lives. Unlike transcendence—that directs us always toward Platonic elsewheres of pure forms, the divine, the heaven, the godhead, rising away from Earth, from the body, corruption, and death—subscendence haunts all of that with the awareness there is only this Earth, "the symbiotic real" that, no matter how hard we try to scrub it off, sticks to us like goo. This awareness takes all of four minutes and thirty-three seconds of silence to establish itself in our lives.

⌀

My friends keep greenhouses on the alluvial fans below the western ramparts of the Wallowa Mountains. Sandy Roth and her husband, Richard Kenton, don't think of themselves as artists, but I would argue that the quality of their attention to the diffuse, slowly accumulating intelligence of plants makes them proponents of a Cagean deference toward silence.

On the summer solstice last year, Sandy and I walked into her greenhouse together at twilight. At that moment, three of the five greenhouses were full of plants grown from seeds or cuttings she and Richard had gathered. On one bench was an incipient savannah of young ponderosa pines, long needles glowing in twilight. On the next bench were a thousand blue spruce. On the next several benches we passed fifty thousand cottonwoods, cuttings of a hundred thousand willows, plush "carpets" of aspen clones, and several benches of red alder. There was also ninebark, syringa, wild rose, snowberry, current, sumac, sage, and bitterbrush. But among this sliver of the diversity of plant life that characterizes our region, we stopped at a bench full of whitebark pines and stood there in silence after the exhaust fans kicked off behind us.

Neither majestic nor widely distributed, the unassuming whitebark pine is a remarkably evolved intelligence. The Forest Service research summary characterizes whitebark pines in eastern Oregon as growing in a narrow ecological niche between seven thousand six hundred and eight thousand five hundred feet. They are the only tree growing at the highest elevations. The oldest trees range between six hundred and a thousand years old. Their habitat is particularly harsh. Deep snowpacks once lasted upward of nine months of the year, and though the growing season along ridge-lines may approach only three months in duration, there is, despite global warming, a persistent chance of frost or snow. The trees prefer cool, moist climates but are also one of the most drought-tolerant species. Though whitebark pines grow in shallow, rocky soils, and often grow on extraordinarily steep slopes, they are able to withstand winds approaching hurricane force. They are not tall trees, seldom surpassing sixty feet, but can be stout. The largest recorded trunk circumference was twenty-seven feet seven inches around. Given the severity of conditions in which whitebark pines live, they often appear battered and broken, sometimes even appearing dead to a casual observer. The tree's life cycle unfolds so slowly that there may still be viable sapwood beneath the thin bark or nearly bare cambium of particularly old trees.

As long ago as 1996, a group of researchers led by Robert E. Keane found a "45 percent decline in whitebark pine cover types in the Columbia River Basin" that is, a 45 percent decline in whitebark pine within stands that are 50 percent or more whitebark pine. Hotter, drier summers and shorter, warmer winters such as we've observed in eastern Oregon over the past thirty years are driving this ancient tree rapidly toward extinction.

Because the whitebark pine seed is "wingless," the tree depends on other species to distribute and disperse its seeds. The whitebark pine lives, therefore, in a cooperative, relational association, an "animal-plant mutualism," with the Clark's nutcracker who caches and eats their seeds. Each is a keystone species in their shared habitat, and many other species within that habitat are likewise dependent on the mutualism of the nutcracker and whitebark. The decline of one can't be separated from the decline of all. We would be fools not to imagine ourselves in a similar mesh of mutualities.

There is one large grove of whitebark pines high in the Lostine River drainage that I visit every summer. The trees are many centuries old and their numbers suggest they dominated that particular site for half a millennium or more. Changes in climate have weakened the trees and made them less able to withstand blister rust, which girdles their trunks and branches, turns the needles brown, then cause the needles to fall. It has been a shocking phenomenon to witness.

Most summers I cross paths with a true mountain lunatic, the composer, translator, and writer Cliff Craigo. We first met on my birthday in the upper Lostine River drainage, during which fevered conversation ensued. At one point, he recited large swaths of Rilke in German. Cliff walks the trails through the Wallowas all summer, going out for as many as five to six weeks at a time, riding his bicycle and pulling a small trailer to a trailhead, where he hides them, then wanders the mountains until he finds his way back to his bike and returns home to Halfway, Oregon. He is witness to the changes affecting the groves of whitebarks and nutcrackers. Having followed this regime for many years, he's compiled a large comparative data set of the effects of climate change. The last we spoke, he had been visiting groves of whitebark in the area of Glacier Peak and Glacier Lake.

There's a popular traverse we've made over the years, climbing the northwest ridge of Eagle Cap Peak, then descending off its southeast flank onto the ridge it shares with Glacier Peak. In the past, we could glissade a thousand feet through the remnant glacier and snowfields to the lake and make a loop hike back to our campsite in the upper Lostine River canyon. By the turn of the century, however, summer snow cover in that basin was spotty at best, and several times we found ourselves descending from the ridge through bare rock and glacial till. Cliff now refers to the area as Lost Glacier Peak and Lost Glacier Lake.

The day we last met along Hurricane Creek, Cliff described the musical composition he hears in his head, a score written on behalf of the dying groves of whitebark pine and their endangered nutcrackers, who have cared for them through millennia. The piece, he said, would be performed on instruments made from the perished trees themselves. These days, any expression of wonder at what is alive but threatened is almost immediately rendered as elegy.

My friend Sandy is no less aware of the fate of these ancient trees that thrived on a cooler, wetter Earth than the one we now live on, but her awareness doesn't elegize. She is determined instead to provide seedlings for those botanists who are trying to figure out how to save this species and its codependent species.

Despite the large number of plants in the greenhouses, what goes on here is directed by concentrated attention to individual lives, many of whom form larger symbiotic associations of mutual interest. My friends are engaged, that is, in a generations-long conversation with these plants about those mutualities. That conversation is focused on what plants know about their changing environment, how they communicate that knowledge, and how we might be guided by such knowledge. No one is more fluent in this language than Sandy. In recent years, she said, plants have "gone into survival mode." Later she explained that as the climate has warmed, seed stratification—replicating the natural conditions that allow plants to germinate after their dormancy, moist-warm or moist-cool—has become increasingly more difficult, requiring our friends in some cases to scarify seed coats in addition to trying to simulate stratification. It's more difficult than ever to germinate whitebark pine seeds.

The trend has been obvious for years. "The plants," Sandy said, "know something big is coming, but it's coming so slowly we don't sense it as clearly as they do." It's a chilling thought, really, to imagine that an entire kingdom of life on our planet is aware of a reality many of us ignore or otherwise try to deny. That plants perceive this reality in a manner more evolved—older, slower, and more subtly attuned to lived reality of the planet—than our own perception of it ought to make us wonder about what else we fail to perceive, as much as what we fail to understand.

"Everything that grows in these greenhouses is a codependent species," Sandy said. "Everything that gets planted out needs those other species the same as those species need these others to survive. This is all I've ever wanted to do with my life: listen to them speak and try to answer."